Establishing Appearances as Divine

Establishing Appearances as Divine

Rongzom Chökyi Zangpo on Reasoning, Madhyamaka, and Purity

by

Heidi I. Köppl

Snow Lion

BOSTON & LONDON

2013

Snow Lion
An imprint of Shambhala Publications, Inc.
Horticultural Hall
300 Massachusetts Avenue
Boston, Massachusetts 02115
www.shambhala.com

9 8 7 6 5 4 3 2 1

FIRST PAPERBACK EDITION
Printed in the United States of America

♾ This edition is printed on acid-free paper that meets the American National Standards Institute Z39.48 Standard.
♻ This book is printed on 30% postconsumer recycled paper.
For more information please visit www.shambhala.com.
Distributed in the United States by Random House, Inc., and in Canada by Random House of Canada Ltd

Designed and typeset by Gopa & Ted2, Inc.

Library of Congress Cataloging-in-Publication Data

Köppl, Heidi I.
Establishing appearances as divine: Rongzom Chökyi Zangpo on reasoning, Madhyamaka, and purity / Heidi I. Köppl.—First Paperback Edition
pages cm
Includes Tibetan text and its English translation.
Includes bibliographical references.
ISBN 978-1-55939-419-2 (paperback)
1. Roṅ-zom Chos-kyi-bzaṅ-po, active 11th century. Gsaṅ sṅags rdo rje theg pa'i tshul las snaṅ ba lhar bsgrub pa. 2. Rñiṅ-ma-pa (Sect)—Doctrines. I. Roṅ-zom Chos-kyi-bzaṅ-po, active 11th century. Gsaṅ sṅags rdo rje theg pa'i tshul las snaṅ ba lhar bsgrub pa. II. Roṅ-zom Chos-kyi-bzaṅ-po, active 11th century. Gsaṅ sṅags rdo rje theg pa'i tshul las snaṅ ba lhar bsgrub pa. English. III. Title.
BQ7662.4.K686 2013
294.3'420423—dc23
2013011556

Table of Contents

Acknowledgments

THE PRESENT WORK could not have come into being without kind help from many sides. First and foremost, I wish to thank Chökyi Nyima Rinpoche who introduced me to pure perception (*dag snang*) as taught in the Nyingma tradition, and who continues to make me aware of its importance and implications. I am thankful also to Khenpo Chöga who inspired me to study the works of Rongzom Chökyi Zangpo and to Khenpo Sherab Zangpo from whom I received lectures and clarifications on *Establishing Appearances as Divine.* To the learned Sakya master Khenpo Ape and the Nyingma Khenchen Padma Sherab, I wish to express my gratitude for their insightful explanations and comments. In general, I would here like to thank everyone at the Kathmandu University Centre for Buddhist Studies and at Ka-Nying Shedrup Ling Monastery, where the Centre is housed, for providing a fertile and three-dimensional environment for my studies. I am indebted also to Christian Wedeymeyer, who as my master's thesis adviser at the University of Copenhagen provided many constructive comments and suggestions for my study of Rongzom and his *Establishing Appearances as Divine.* I likewise thank Andreas Doctor for much helpful advice during the various stages of my work. To Georges Dreyfus, John Makransky, and José Cabezón I am most grateful for their constructive critique and kind encouragement, and I wish to thank Gene Smith for his insightful comments on the genealogy of the editions of *Establishing Appearances as Divine.* I would also like to thank my friends James Gentry, Douglas Duckworth, Adam Pearcey, and Cortland Dahl for their beneficial feedback. Last but not least, this work owes much to the perceptive suggestions and loving support of my husband, Thomas Doctor.

Introduction

TRANSFORMATION not only of one's identity but also one's environment is an important principle of Buddhist esoteric philosophy. In esoteric scriptures one is instructed to visualize oneself as a deity (*lha, devatā*),[1] a divine identity who resides in a perfect sphere (*dkyil 'khor, maṇḍala*), and through repeatedly training in that one will finally perfect the transformation and become the deity itself. However, one may wonder whether sentient beings are held to be intrinsically pure (*dag pa*) and divine, or whether they merely become purified by the visualization of purity? Is the practice of deity yoga merely a means (*thabs, upāya*), or is it more fundamentally connected to the nature of things? These questions appear to have been among the main concerns of Rongzom Chökyi Zangpo,[2] a proponent of the Early Translations (*snga 'gyur*)[3] who was active in Tibet during the eleventh century, when he composed a concise treatise on this topic called *Establishing Appearances as Divine*. The text's fascinating objective consists in establishing appearances as divine by means of mahāyānic reasoning. In the following, we shall investigate Rongzom's philosophy of purity, along with his assessment and application of reasoning, with special reference to this text. Subsequently I present a translation of *Establishing Appearances as Divine* itself. The translation is accompanied by a comparative edition of the Tibetan text.

Chapter 1 offers a brief introductory description of Rongzom's career, his works, and environment, as his philosophy cannot be properly understood in complete separation from the unique spiritual environment that prevailed during the eleventh century in Tibet.[4]

While studying Rongzom's works, one quickly notices his outspoken critique of the Madhyamaka, which is evidence of his preference for the esoteric view. Many Tibetan philosophers have treated the Madhyamaka as the perfect view in both the Sūtra and Mantra contexts, and among modern Nyingma scholars the issue of the superior view is often downplayed in general discourse. One may thus be surprised to witness Rongzom argue vehemently for an esoteric view that clearly is elevated above the Madhyamaka. In chapter 2, I consider the positions of later Nyingma scholars regarding the views in Sūtra and Mantra to establish whether Rongzom is unique in advocating this clear and uncompromising preference. In particular, I am concerned with the views of Longchen Rabjam (1308-1362),[5] Lochen Dharma Śrī (1654-1718),[6] 'Ju Mipham (1846-1912),[7] and the latter's commentator, Do-ngag Tenpay Nyima (1895/1900-1959).[8]

It should be noted that as chapter 2 constitutes a concentrated study of the notion of view, it leaves aside discussions of some broader issues, such as the cultural-historical developments surrounding the terms "Sūtra" and "Mantra," and the way in which Mantra, on occasion, has been considered a supplementary teaching to Sūtra, and at other times a vehicle (*theg pa, yāna*) in its own right. It must also be mentioned that the terms "Sūtra" and "Mantra" are used in this work in a way that conforms with the general Tibetan use of the terms *mdo* (Sūtra) and *sngags* (Mantra) as referring to two distinct levels of Buddhist doctrine, and not, therefore, with the use of such terms in the Indian Buddhist context. With regard to the superiority of the esoteric view, except for Padmasambhava's *Garland of Views as Oral Instructions*[9] and the *Guhyagarbha Tantra*, no pre-Rongzom sources were consulted in detail. While an investigation into the origins of the notion of a superior esoteric view would clearly be a fruitful topic for a future study, the present work is primarily concerned with Rongzom's own opinions on the issue and their influence on later representatives of the Nyingma tradition.

Regarding the use of reasoning on the esoteric level, I have studied the Nyingma masters mentioned above to determine whether Rongzom's application of dialectical tools on the esoteric level represented a unique, idiosyncratic approach or whether it had obtained a wider impact on the Nyingma history of ideas in general. A number of Nyingma scholars did in fact find it appropriate, if not outright obligatory, to set forth reasonings similar to Rongzom's for the establishment of a superior esoteric view and the notion of purity. The nature of these reasonings and their implications for Nyingma esoteric exegesis present themselves as particularly fruitful fields for future research.

Establishing Appearances as Divine is usually described in the present-day Nyingma tradition as a commentary on the *Guhyagarbha Tantra.* If one accepts this classification, it would lend further testimony to Rongzom's general fondness for the *Guhyagarbha* teachings and his attempt to validate these teachings through the style of discourse usually associated with the classical dialectical approach. Considering that the initial thesis of *Establishing Appearances as Divine* follows almost verbatim that of Padmasambhava in his *Garland of Views as Oral Instructions,*[10] a treatise that itself is based on the *Guhyagarbha,*[11] one may reasonably conclude that the traditional classification of *Establishing Appearances as Divine* as a text pertaining to the Mahāyoga class of Tantra is valid.[12] Therefore, as a starting point for my investigations it seemed appropriate to delineate Rongzom's use of esoteric doxographical models. Rongzom often categorizes Mantra through the twofold division of external Mantra (*sngags phyi pa*) and internal Mantra (*sngags nang pa*), as well as the ninefold set of vehicles (*theg pa rim pa dgu*). His doxographical model differs in certain regards from that employed by later Nyingma masters, such as Longchen Rabjam. Over time a tendency developed to correlate or even equate the Nyingma esoteric models employed by Rongzom with those of the New (*gsar ma*) Schools. Chapter 2 includes a description of Rongzom's doxographical apparatus and a brief introduction to Nyingma and New Schools models in general. A valuable secondary source in this context was Germano's treatment of the development of the "seminal heart" (*snying thig*).[13]

In this way chapter 2 considers a diversity of views that are all attributed to so-called Nyingma philosophers. A number of commonalities do indeed indicate a homogeneous tradition in support of such a unified philosophical approach. However, when studying the views of individual philosophers who themselves may be separated by centuries, one must be careful not to construct an overly simplified and somewhat fanciful image of a fully homologous school of thought. The present work, for instance, makes use of the terms "suddenist" (*cig car ba*) and "gradualist" (*rim gyis pa*).[14] Although one may find a suddenist tendency in the writings of Rongzom[15] and several other central Nyingma proponents, it is also noteworthy that the prominent Zur clan was explicit in promoting the teaching of the *Guhyagarbha Tantra* as a gradual path.[16] Thus, although chapter 2 identifies certain trends common to a general Nyingma school of thought, and although one may therefore speak of a particular "Nyingma perspective," I hope this will not lead readers to develop ideas of a clear-cut and monolithic tradition. Let us instead simply acknowledge the presence of certain common currents of thought in the works of otherwise diverse authors.

During my research it became clear that Rongzom shows his preference for the esoteric view and his commitment to the principle of purity most explicitly through comparing the views of Mantra and Madhyamaka. Since the Madhyamaka school is a primary reference point for Rongzom as he posits the superior view of Mantra, it is relevant to determine what type of Madhyamaka philosophy Rongzom describes in his works. In short, it seemed that to understand Rongzom's treatment of the esoteric view I would need to investigate his Madhyamaka exegesis, as this is his primary negative reference when setting forth the superior view of Mantra.[17] For that reason, chapter 3 investigates Rongzom's Madhyamaka exegesis and critique.[18] This section also examines the influence of Rongzom's Madhyamaka on his professed follower, Mipham, whose interpretations of both exoteric and esoteric Buddhism play a crucial role in modern day Nyingma exegesis and who most surprisingly, given Rongzom's vehement critique of the Madhyamaka and his silence on the Svātantrika/Prāsaṅgika distinction, claims to base his Prāsaṅgika view on Rongzom's analysis. The post-Mipham Nyingma tradition values Rongzom as a source of supreme authority and tends to interpret him with continuous recourse to Mipham's exegetical models. With this in mind, chapter 3 compares the views of Rongzom and Mipham in order to investigate the unique traits of their individual approaches and to estimate the extent of Rongzom's influence on Mipham. With respect to Mipham's Madhyamaka, this study relies primarily on his *Beacon of Certainty*[19] and *Speech of Delight*.[20] Chapter 3 has two major objectives: (1) to explore and delineate Rongzom's view on Madhyamaka on his own terms, as much as possible, and (2) to establish a hermeneutical link between Rongzom's criticisms of Madhyamaka and his treatment of the esoteric theorem of purity.

In chapter 4, the role of reasoning and the four principles in Rongzom's writings are treated and his views are compared to the *Saṁdhinirmocanasūtra* (a locus classicus of the four reasonings), the *Abhidharmasamuccaya*, and an early Tibetan *pramāṇa* source[21] attributed to the eighth-century Tibetan king Trisong Deutsen.[22] Both Mipham and post-Mipham perspectives on the reasonings are occasionally addressed to analyze differences between Rongzom's presentations and what appears to be the current position in Nyingma exegesis.[23]

Rongzom's treatment of the four reasonings appears unconventional even in a Nyingma context, and he is ambiguous with respect to reasoning itself. I argue that Mipham's *pramāṇa* system presents an original and innovative interpretation of Rongzom. In the final section of chapter 4, the epistemological and hermeneutical implications of this system, which has become a hallmark of modern day Nyingma exegesis, is briefly examined.[24] The use of sūtric principles of reasoning and a specific *pramāṇa* for the establishment of purity are indicators of the deep philosophical importance with which the Nyingma school invests this principle.

For the translation of *Establishing Appearances as Divine* I have sought to highlight and comment on particularly complex passages through a limited number of annotations. Often my comments simply take the form of references to relevant passages in the preceding chapters. Although a terse and pregnant text like this obviously invites much further annotation, it is my hope that the present rudimentary commentary may be an unassuming but helpful companion during readings of the text.

With these introductory remarks in mind let us now turn to a discussion of our main protagonist, Rongzom Chökyi Zangpo.

· 1 ·

Rongzom's Environment, Life, and Works

To begin this study, it will be helpful to contextualize Rongzom through a brief description of the spiritual environment of the eleventh century. Given the skeptical attitude toward the Nyingma tantras (*rgyud rnying ma*) that prevailed in many circles during that century, we can understand Rongzom as an advocate of the Early Translations who was active in a rather hostile yet also intellectually inspiring environment. The following discussion will also offer some observations regarding Rongzom's literary style, particularly his occasional lack of conformity with literary conventions.

Rongzom lived in a time that was marked, politically, by the decentralization of the government and, spiritually, by a reexamination of the Buddhist heritage that found its way into Tibet during the imperial period. Seemingly discontented with the existing spiritual situation in Tibet, many scholars and adepts turned to India for inspiration. The consequence of this renewed surge of interest in India as the primary source of authentic Buddhism was the proliferation of diverse practice lineages, which, as far as they continued to exist, later became known as the New Schools. In the face of this new influx of practice material, the Nyingma school found itself hard pressed to demonstrate the authenticity of its tantras and, in the evolving propagation of the New Schools, criticism against the Nyingma tantras intensified. The decentralization of the governing body in Tibet brought with it the state's inability to control the influx and proliferation of spiritual literature in Tibet, and thus Rongzom's time is characterized by the emergence of a diversity of schools of thought and religious practice.[25] At the same time the edicts by King Photreng Shiway Ö[26] and by Lha Lama Yeshe Ö[27] bear evidence of a general critical attitude against certain tantras and tantric practices.

In this spiritual climate, which quite freely absorbed Indian spiritual subject matter and yet often was critical of the texts and practices of the Nyingma school, Rongzom considered methods to advocate and prove the validity of the Nyingma tantras that were under attack. In his commentary on the *Guhyagarbha Tantra* Rongzom even promotes the tradition of the Early Translations by means of an identification of "six distinctions" through which the school achieves superiority when compared to the New Schools.[28]

Although the term "Nyingmapa" implies "The Old School," i.e., those adhering primarily to the tantras transmitted during the imperial period, the spiritual innovation taking place during the eleventh century did not stop at the school's doorstep. An innovative and profound change within the Nyingma came about through the appearance of the "seminal heart" (*snying thig*) scriptures as part of the emergence of "treasure" (*gter ma*) literature.[29] Over the years these teachings were to become so dominant in Tibet that they became almost synonymous with the Dzogchen teachings.[30] In this way the transmission of texts within the Nyingma context was resumed and revitalized during the period of the Later Dissemination (*phyi dar*) by the controversial unearthing of many hidden treasure texts (*gter ma*). Traditionally, even Rongzom himself is claimed to have discovered a number of such treasures although, according to Jamgon Kongtrul,[31] none of these texts have survived.[32]

While various biographies of Rongzom are still extant, they all appear to be based on two accounts by his students Yol Genyen Dorje Wangchug[33] and Gyag Dorje Dzinpa Chenpo.[34] The exact dates for Rongzom's life are still to be determined. Rongzom is said to have met Atīśa (982-1054) upon the latter's arrival in Tibet.[35] According to his students' accounts, Rongzom grew up in lower Tsang and, although a lay practitioner, he became an erudite scholar and the author of numerous treatises on philosophy, epistemology, history, rituals, grammar, and even topics such as husbandry and farming.[36] Rongzom is said to have authored works comprising one hundred thousand *ślokas*, or more than sixty volumes.[37] The earliest index[38] of his works was produced by his disciple Rongpa Mepung,[39] who enumerates more than 360 works,[40] yet many of the titles listed appear to have been lost. Among his extant works, the most renowned are his *Commentary on the Guhyagarbha Tantra*, the first full-fledged Tibetan commentary on this text,[41] and *Entering the Way of the Great Vehicle*, which seeks to present the diversity of Buddhist teaching in the light of a Dzogchen critique.[42] In the colophon to *Establishing Appearances as Divine* we see this text specified as being the "greater version," thus indicating that there existed other versions of this text.[43] In Rongpa Mepung's index this text is listed as "*Establishment of Appearances as Divine,* known as the seven [texts] of various lengths,"[44] which indicates the existence of an original set of seven versions and highlights how important the issue of establishing the divine purity of all appearances must have been to Rongzom. Today, the only extant version appears to be the "long" (*chen po*) text.

Often viewed by modern scholarship as an apologist for the Nyingma tradition, Rongzom achieved a landmark status for his philosophical works among later Nyingma scholars, especially Mipham.[45] During his time, Rongzom apparently became known not just for his vast knowledge of spiritual matters but also for his translation abilities.[46] However, according to his biographies, Rongzom was also criticized for composing religious treatises without possessing the proper qualifications. Perhaps in Rongzom's day the general perception was that Tibetans were supposed to translate Indian sources into Tibetan and not "fabricate" by producing texts of their own. Rongzom's hagiographies present accounts of his meeting with Atīśa, and likewise speak of him encountering masters such as Gö Khugpa Lhetse[47] (eleventh century) and the famous translator Marpa (1012-1097), student of the Indian yogin adept Nāropa.[48] The two latter spiritual figures had approached Rongzom to rebuke him for his irresponsible authorship, yet upon meeting him they ended up expressing admiration rather than contempt.[49] To what degree these reported meetings with famous opponents have any historical reality is hard to estimate, yet the accounts are interesting as they underscore an atmosphere of tension and a quest for authenticity. In any case, the period is certainly characterized by an utter reliance on India and things Indian for the establishment of spiritual validity. Displaying one's strict reliance on Indian scriptures thus became especially important for philosophers of the eleventh century.[50]

In certain regards, Rongzom does not fit into this pattern of strict adherence to Indian roots, rules, and practices. In nearly all of Rongzom's writings, the traditional initial homage that one finds in Buddhist treatises, whether Indian or Tibetan, is missing.[51] One may wonder why an acclaimed scholar such as Rongzom would omit this important facet in his writings. Was Rongzom's style of composition in vogue during his time? Certainly not.[52] The opening of Rongzom's *Entering the Way of the Great Vehicle* begins abruptly with the statement, "Just [a few] points spoken on the manner in which one enters the Mahāyāna way."[53] *Entering the Way of the Great*

Vehicle is one of Rongzom's most voluminous extant compositions, and it is therefore interesting that he gives an appearance of wanting to say just a few words on the topic. Rongzom was clearly aware of established etiquette, as his treatise on linguistics, the *Commentary to the Weapon of Speech* (*Smra sgo mtshon cha'i 'grel*), notes that "to begin [a Buddhist treatise], one pays homage in order to eliminate obstacles and follow the very best of customs."[54] However, Rongzom refrains from paying such homage in almost all of his extant treatises. These omissions of an homage lend a sense of bluntness and directness to his style.

Another interesting trait in Rongzom's writings is that he—to my knowledge—never claims his discussions are repetitions of previous statements of the Buddha or masters of the past—a measure commonly employed by traditional scholars to underscore the validity of their writings. Especially during the eleventh century, with all its debates over authenticity, such an approach would seem sensible for anyone wishing a common acceptance of one's writings. Yet Rongzom appears to have been unconcerned with concealing any sense of "private production" (*rang bzo*) in his works.[55] Rongzom also reportedly criticized certain Indians visiting Tibet for frivolously writing their treatises only to cater to Tibetans and their particular, culturally determined likes and dislikes.[56] In this way, he may have been objecting indirectly to matters of ethnicity and geography becoming instrumental for the validation of Dharma. As a whole, Rongzom's style of writing gives the impression of an outspoken and undaunted character.

Rongzom's compositions also bear evidence of the changes occurring to Tibet's spiritual landscape during the eleventh century. His exegetical enterprise abounds with logico-epistemological structures, and makes frequent use of Sanskrit terms. While these features of Rongzom's writings certainly indicate a concern with deflecting criticism against the Nyingma school, they are likewise symptomatic of the spirit of the eleventh century. This period witnessed a surge in interest in Buddhist logic and epistemology, and saw the development of what we may call Tibetan scholasticism.[57] This Zeitgeist seems not to have evaded Rongzom, as he enthusiastically emphasizes tools of reasoning in the process of validation.[58] Sangphu (Gsang phu) Monastery in Central Tibet (founded 1071 or 1073) was emerging as a major center for philosophical learning and debate, and this institution may have had considerable influence on Rongzom. In any case, the tools of persuasion employed in *Establishing Appearances as Divine* express the scholastic emphasis on valid means of cognition (*tshad ma, pramāṇa*) that is a characteristic of the eleventh century. The dialogue between two opposing parties in *Establishing Appearances as Divine* is likewise indicative of the period's scholastic tensions between philosophers favoring either a gradual or sudden path.

Skepticism towards the Ancient Tantras may have inspired Rongzom to employ the very dialectical tools that were in vogue during the eleventh century and were favored by his opponents, tools that could automatically produce an air of authority and authenticity. However, to attribute his dialectical evaluations of Vajrayāna themes exclusively to such a strategic concern—the simple wish to furnish credibility to otherwise contested Nyingma esoteric themes—would be to overlook Rongzom's keen interest in Mahāyāna discourse in general. His enthusiastic adoption of dialectical methods also suggests that he was genuinely inspired by the emerging Tibetan scholastic movement. Nevertheless, Rongzom occasionally expressed profound reservations about the purview of reasoning, an ambiguity we will pursue in detail in chapter 4.

In summary, Rongzom was active during a time of spiritual diversity. This period, when a great influx of new Buddhist textual material was absorbed into Tibet, was a time of an increasingly skeptical attitude towards the tantras imported during the early dissemination. Rongzom's style of writing reflects this culturally enriched environment. It combines the experiential perspective of Dzogchen and Tantra with elements of classical dialectical Indian Buddhist scholarship in a format shaped by eristic concerns. With these preliminary impressions of our author and his text, let us now proceed with a study of the Nyingma notion of Mantrayāna to provide a philosophical context for the notion of purity.

· 2 ·

Introduction to Mantra from a Nyingma Perspective

RONGZOM, as a proponent of the Early Translations, was decidedly a tantrika, a trait that becomes fully evident in works such as *Establishing Appearances as Divine*. Since this text is traditionally classified as pertaining to Mahāyoga, it may be useful to provide a doxographical sketch highlighting the role of the Mahāyoga within the general doxographical structures. We will therefore discuss Mahāyoga in the Nyingma esoteric tradition and briefly contrast the general doxographical system of this tradition to that of the New Schools. We will also compare Rongzom's explanations of the external and internal Tantrayāna to those of Longchen Rabjam who, active three centuries later, adopted a hermeneutical approach more closely related to the exegetical models of the New Schools. The comparisons with Longchen Rabjam will introduce us to the recurring theme of the "inseparability of the two truths" (*bden gnyis dbyer med*), which for Rongzom as well as for later Nyingma masters holds great importance in the esoteric context.

The Sūtra teachings are often said to be distinguished from Tantra in their application of dialectical tools. Yet dialectical reasoning also plays a considerable role as an exegetical method on the esoteric level for Nyingma scholars and Rongzom is indeed not alone in attempting to establish esoteric principles through reasoning. Likewise, many Nyingma masters hold the Mantra view to be superior to that of Sūtra because of its perceived subtler and more complete comprehension of the inseparabilty of the two truths. We will survey differences in the view (*lta ba, darśana*) of Sūtra and Mantra as espoused by prominent Nyingma masters in the final part of chapter 2. This will serve as a preliminary to the more lengthy treatment of Rongzom's own position in the following chapters.[59]

2.1 A Comparison of Esoteric Systems

The Mahāyoga tantras, imported from India to Tibet during the eighth and ninth centuries, constituted mainstream tantras for the Nyingmapas in the same way that the *Anuttarayogatantras (*rnal 'byor bla med*) became central for the proponents of the New Schools. The latter tradition, i.e., the Sakya (Sa skya), Kagyu (Bka' brgyud), and Gelug (Dge lugs) schools, classify their tantras into four sections:

"Action" (*bya ba*, Kriyā)
"Conduct" (*spyod pa*, Caryā)
"Union" (*rnal 'byor*, Yoga)
"Unexcelled Union" (*rnal 'byor bla med*, *Anuttarayogatantra)[60]

This doxographical tradition of classifying the tantras into four sections only penetrated Tibet during the eleventh century.[61] The importation of the Nyingma tantras, on the other hand, is said to have taken place during the seventh to tenth centuries. The Nyingma school treats all its six classifications of Tantra as distinct vehicles (*theg pa, yāna*),[62] so that when adding these six to the three sūtric vehicles—those of Listeners (*nyan thos*), Self-realized Buddhas (*rang rgyal*), and Bodhisattvas (*byang chub sems dpa'*) —altogether nine vehicles are enumerated. This enumeration prompted criticism by other schools arguing that only three distinct vehicles exist.[63] Furthermore, the six esoteric classifications of the Nyingma are divided into the "external Tantrayāna of Capacity" (*phyi pa thub pa'i rgyud kyi theg pa*),[64] to which the first three classes of Tantra belong, and the "internal Tantrayāna of Skillful Means" (*nang pa thabs kyi rgyud kyi theg pa*), consisting of the latter three:

Kriyā (*bya ba*)
Ubhayā (*gnyis ka*)[65]
Yoga (*rnal 'byor*)
Mahāyoga (*rnal 'byor chen po*)
Anuyoga (*rjes su rnal 'byor*)
Atiyoga (*bshin tu rnal 'byor*)

The three lower tantra sections of the New and the Old Schools are often described as being similar in emphasis and approach.[66] There seem, however, to be considerable differences between the two traditions. As can be seen in the expositions of Rongzom and Lochen Dharma Śrī,[67] proponents of the Early Translations assert that, even in the context of the outer sections of Tantra, conventional appearances are considered pure, a point of criticism by Sapaṇ in his *Clear Differentiation of the Three Codes.*[68] Likewise, although similarities in content exist between the three higher, or inner, tantra classifications of the Nyingma and the *Anuttarayogatantra of the New Schools, it would be problematic to equate them.[69] Even though certain Nyingma masters, especially Longchen Rabjam, equated the Nyingma doxographical models with those of the New Schools, they may well have done so as part of an effort to establish the authenticity of the Nyingma tantras.[70] As well as the obvious difference in their period of reception in Tibet, the two traditions generally differ with regard to the sources of transmission from diverse geographical locations outside of Tibet and the intervening development of received traditions in Tibet during the four centuries prior to the reception of the esoteric transmission of the New Schools.[71]

In his explanation of the esoteric systems, Rongzom never operates with the doxographical model of the New Schools, but mostly relies on a general division into external and internal Tantrayāna. In this he differs from later Nyingma scholars who frequently synchronized the nine vehicles with the four tantra sections of the New Schools. In the *Commentary to the Garland of Views as Oral Instructions,* Rongzom classifies the three higher tantras as "internal Tantrayāna of skillful means" (*rnal 'byor nang pa thabs kyi rgyud kyi theg pa*) and divides the view into "the way of generation" (*bskyed pa'i tshul*), "the way of perfection" (*rdzogs pa'i tshul*), and "the way of great perfection" (*rdzogs pa chen po'i tshul*).[72] Elsewhere in the same text, Rongzom explains that "the way of generation" (*bskyed pa'i tshul*) refers to Mahāyoga, but he does not explicitly identify the other two traditions (*tshul*) as Anu and Ati.[73] Interestingly, in *Entering the Way of the Great Vehicle* Rongzom does not divide the tantras in terms of external and internal, but divides Yoga into the four sections of Yoga, Mahāyoga, Anuyoga, and Atiyoga. He explains that these four aspects of Yoga generally accord in emphasizing the "yoga of the internal mind" (*nang sems kyi rnal 'byor*), after which he points out their differences.[74]

In his commentary on the *Guhyagarbha,* Rongzom divides the Secret Mantra into only three vehicles, i.e., Caryā, Ubhayā, and Yoga. Yet immediately afterwards he remarks that there is also the tradition of categorizing the teachings into nine vehicles, as done in the *Garland of Views as Oral Instruction*. In his *Commentary to the*

Garland of Views as Oral Instructions, Rongzom briefly elaborates on the difference between the external and internal Tantrayāna:

> As for the external yoga, the capacity tantra, briefly, it is generally set forth as external with reference to its view and conduct. Regarding its view, oneself and the Buddha are not regarded as equal on the relative level. Regarding its conduct, there is no practice of the yogic discipline of equality. As for the sense of capacity, this refers to the inability to practice the samayas which are not to be observed, and [this practice] is thus not free from the ordinary vows. The internal tantra of skillful means is the opposite of that. One regards oneself as the unmistaken Maheśvara and practices the yogic discipline of equality. Even though nothing is prohibited with regard to the conduct of the three doors, one is unstained by faults and therefore skilled in method.[75]

The classification of phenomena with reference to two truths is not only applied in the Sūtrayāna, but can also be found in the esoteric teachings. In the Nyingma school, a prominent esoteric explanation of the two-truths paradigm is the inseparability of the "two superior truths" (*lhag pa'i bden pa gnyis*),[76] i.e., great purity (*dag pa chen po*) as the relative truth (*kun rdzob den pa, saṃvṛtisatya*) and great equality (*mnyams pa chen po*) as the ultimate truth (*don dam den pa, paramārthasatya*). Often this is pointed out as the defining view of Mahāyoga (*rnal 'byor chen po*). More generally, the tradition also tends to differentiate the view of the esoteric teachings as a whole from that of the sūtric teachings by ascribing a full realization of the inseparability of the two truths to the estoric teachings alone.

Longchen Rabjam, in the *Treasury of Philosophical Tenets* and elsewhere, differentiates the external from the internal tantras through their capacity to recognize the inseparability of the two truths: "First with regard to the distinction of the view, the external [tantra] views the two truths as different, while the internal [tantra] views them as inseparable. With regard to meditation, the external does not meditate on deity yoga, while the internal does. With regard to conduct, the external practices pure conduct and is not capable of relying on the five types of meat, etc., whereas the internal is."[77]

It appears that Rongzom generally ascribes such recognition to the lower tantras also. For instance, in *Entering the Way of the Great Vehicle,* he proclaims, "Although there are those internal differences in the Secret Mantra, the assertion of the two truths being inseparable starts with Kriyā and is perfected in the Great Perfection."[78]

In the concise *Black Snake Discourse,*[79] Rongzom likewise considers the inseparability of the two truths to be a feature of the lower tantras. While the external Tantrayāna possesses an inferior realization of this inseparability, the internal is endowed with a medium realization, and only the Great Perfection is fully capable of realizing it. (Interestingly Rongzom here seems to classify the Great Perfection as not belonging to the internal tantras.) Although he qualifies the inseparability of the two truths in the external tantra as limited, he does contend that it is partly realized and thus his position on the view of the external and internal tantra appears to differ from that of Longchen Rabjam.

Both Rongzom and Longchen Rabjam on several occasions draw the dividing line between the general categories of Sūtra and Mantra precisely with reference to the view of the inseparability of the two truths. Therefore, taking into account Longchen Rabjam's explanation that the external tantras do not realize the inseparability of the two truths, we may surmise that when certain Nyingma scholars point out the difference in view between Sūtra and Mantra, the term "Mantra" at times refers exclusively to the three higher tantras of the Nyingma system.[80]

This outlines the different esoteric models followed by the New and Old Schools and roughly displays the models of thought that Rongzom adhered to. For the Nyingmas, and especially for Rongzom, the inseparability of the two truths is of vital importance in the esoteric context and, as we shall see below, for Rongzom the progression of the six esoteric vehicles is highly dependent on the degree of realization of the inseparability of the two truths.

2.2 The Relationship between Sūtra and Mantra in the Nyingma School

2.2.1 Use of Sūtric Terms in Esoteric Writings

The abundance of dialectical features in the Sūtrayāna might lead one to believe that only this vehicle uses a dialectical approach to the two-truths notion, while the Secret Mantrayāna puts little emphasis on establishing the nature of the two truths philosophically. Thus many proponents of the New Schools argue that the only difference between Sūtrayāna and Mantrayāna lies in the domain of skillful means and not the view. For most proponents of the New Schools, the perfect view has already been espoused in the teachings of Madhyamaka, accessed with the help of various logical arguments. Hence there is no need for separate discourse on view, tenets (*grub mtha', siddhānta*), etc. at the level of the esoteric teachings. However, the two-truths system is a prominent feature of the Nyingma tantras and their esoteric tradition, as is the application of dialectical tools[81] to resolve the purity and equality of all phenomena. For instance, the commentaries on the *Guhyagarbha Tantra*, the root tantra of the Mahāyoga tantras, teach how to resolve the nature of phenomena through "arguments of the four realizations" (*rtogs pa bzhi'i gtan tshigs*).[82] Jamgon Kongtrul, in his *Treasury of Knowledge,*[83] further summarizes different arguments of the Mahāyoga tradition through which one gains access to purity, equality, and the inseparable nature of the two truths: the argument of the three purities (*dag pa gsum gyi gtan tshigs*), the argument of the four equalities (*mnyam pa bzhi'i gtan tshigs*), and the argument of great identity (*bdag nyid chen po'i gtan tshigs*). An early text which makes elaborate use of reasoning is the *Sprout of Secret Mantra,*[84] a terma (*gter ma*) revealed by the terton (*gter ston*) Nyangral Nyimay Özer[85] (1124-1192). Even Sapaṇ mentions, in the *Clear Differentiation of the Three Codes,* that "the nature of the three purities is expounded in the Mahāyoga tantras, and one should learn well the citations, reasoning, and instructions [regarding these three purities] from one's master."[86] Although further research in this area is needed, a logical establishment of purity, as provided by Rongzom, is not an unusual procedure for an advocate of the Early Translations.[87] Rongzom's proof of purity nevertheless differs from the standard logical arguments because the tools of reasoning used to establish the esoteric view in *Establishing Appearances as Divine* are all well known sūtric principles of reasoning. We shall return to this topic below; at this point let us simply note that the two truths, and their ascertainment through reasoning, have a well established use in the Nyingma esoteric tradition.

2.2.2 The Superiority of Mantra According to the Nyingma School

For the remaining part of this section, we will focus on the way that the Nyingma school traditionally has held the esoteric view as superior to the sūtric view. Although our concern will mainly be with Nyingma authors, we shall also briefly examine the views of Tsongkhapa and Sapaṇ as representatives of the New Schools. We will attempt to present a general Nyingma outlook on Tantra to contextualize the subsequent discussion of Rongzom's critique of Madhyamaka and his preference for the esoteric notion of purity. Let us first consider the influential Nyingma master of the sixteenth century Lochen Dharma Śrī, who in his *Speech of the Lord of Secrets* describes the difference between the Pāramitā vehicle and Mantra in the following way: "All the ancient masters explain that they differ in whether they are capable of taking the relative onto the path. In the Pāramitā vehicle, the ultimate is something to be achieved while the relative is something to be abandoned. Since, according to Mantra, even with respect to the relative all phenomena are experienced as equality, they are not abandoned but taken as the path. Hence, the two truths are [here] not partial and are therefore superior [to those of the Pāramitā vehicle]."[88]

Lochen Dharma Śrī's differentiation is noteworthy in claiming that this classification stems from ancient masters, among whom Rongzom is presumably included, and in denying the Pāramitā vehicle a realization of the equality of the two truths.[89] Moreover, by making the outlook and conduct regarding relative truth the dividing line between Sūtra and Mantra, Dharma Śrī explains that the two esoteric truths are superior because they possess the same veridical value. The relative as purity is equal to the ultimate and hence there is nothing impure to be abandoned.[90]

In the *Precious Wish-fulfilling Treasury*, Longchen Rabjam explains the difference between the dialectical and the Mantra vehicles in a somewhat similar manner.[91] His explanations underscore the Sūtrayāna's alleged lack of realization of the inseparability of the two truths, lack of understanding of the outer and inner phenomena as pure divinities, etc. In Longchen Rabjam's *Treasury of Philosophical Tenets*, we find a statement that further underscores discrepancies between the esoteric and the Madhyamaka views that are similar to those we will see Rongzom describe: "While the dialectical view merely realizes emptiness, the freedom from mental constructs, [it] does not realize the inseparability of the two truths, the primordial nature abiding as divinities and mantras. Mantra [however] realizes it."[92]

Interestingly, Longchen Rabjam seems to imply that there is a view higher than the view of emptiness (*stong pa nyid, śūnyatā*), the freedom from all mental constructs. This issue has also been addressed by both Sapaṇ and Mipham. Sapaṇ, in his *Clear Differentiation of the Three Codes,* strongly challenges the idea of a Mantrayāna view that is superior to freedom from mental constructs,[93] and for Sapaṇ there are therefore no higher views to be discovered beyond the Madhyamaka in the context of analytical study:[94] "Thus all views belonging to the level of learning are in agreement from the Madhyamaka upward."[95]

As a follower of the nonsectarian (*ris med*) movement, Mipham at times minimizes the discrepancies between Sapaṇ's statement and the general Nyingma outlook on Mantra. In his *Beacon of Certainty,* for instance, Mipham explains, "The Great Madhyamaka, freedom from all [mental] constructs, and the Great Perfection, luminosity, have [different] names, [yet] are identical in meaning. There is no view superior to that, for without apprehending appearance and emptiness in alternation this is the freedom from the [mental] constructs of the four extremes. Anything else would become possessed of [mental] constructs."[96]

In this way he agrees in his *Beacon of Certainty* with Sapaṇ that there cannot be a view higher than that of freedom from mental constructs. What Mipham refers to in this passage is a view that does not in any way perceive appearance and emptiness as separate, in other words, a view that realizes the inseparable unity of the two truths. Mipham's statement is therefore still in agreement with earlier Nyingma descriptions of the superior esoteric view.[97] Elsewhere Mipham is explicit in asserting the view of Mantra as vastly superior to that taught in the sūtras.[98]

For the Nyingma scholars there is a further feature that distinguishes the Sūtra view from that of Mantra. Do-ngag Tenpay Nyima explains, "[Let us consider] the difference between the views of Sūtra and Mantra [in the light of] their secret key point and final significance. This can well [be understood] in terms of the difference between a gradual process of gaining access to unity free from all [mental] constructs and an instantaneous perfection of the distinctive, profound view of the supreme absence of conflict between appearance and emptiness."[99] This statement underscores a hallmark of the Nyingma school: its advocating a suddenist path. In chapter 3 we will examine this feature in the light of Mipham's propagation of the Madhyamaka and Rongzom's critique of the same.

The Nyingma notion of a superior view of Mantra contrasts sharply with the view of Tsongkhapa, who consistently argues that the view of Mantra is nothing but Prāsaṅgika.[100] In *The Stages of Mantra,*[101] he describes the difference between Sūtra and Mantra in the following way: "Generally, one must not determine the difference between the small and the great vehicle in terms of the knowledge of emptiness, [but] in terms of method. In particular, regarding the differentiation of the great vehicle into two, the difference must also not be determined in terms of the knowledge that realizes the profound, but in terms of method."[102] Tsongkhapa's follower Khedrup likewise maintains that, "the view of all the sections of Tantra is the Prāsaṅgika."[103]

As we have seen, the different schools of Buddhism in Tibet propagated different interpretations of the nature of, and relationship between, the views of Sūtra and Mantra. For some advocates of the Early Translations, the relative and the absolute are of equal veridical value; thus the relative as divinities must be the object of realization just as much as the ultimate equality is. Seen in this light, the emptiness *qua* freedom from all mental constructs advocated by the Madhyamaka as the supreme view, put simply, lacks divine appearances as the relative truth. In the Nyingma tradition, divine appearances can be the natural expression of the luminous nature of the mind.[104] According to this position, by negating such appearances, the natural expression of luminosity, one ends up with an ultimate truth that is a barren negation, emptiness isolated from its inherent radiance, and the two truths would thus be unreasonably and unnaturally separated. While the Nyingma philosophers that we have visited here may differ in their individual ways of juxtaposing or reconciling the views of Sūtra and Mantra, they all agree that in the final analysis a separation between the two truths is untenable.

To sum up, some Nyingma masters identify the discrepancy between Sūtra and Mantra in the sūtric vehicle's failure to realize the inseparability of the two truths. Other Nyingma thinkers point to the Sūtra system's lack of realization of the equal veridical value of the two truths. Some commentators determine an absence of pure divinities/luminosity in Sūtra, while others see a failure to provide a sudden approach to the realization of the nature of appearance and emptiness.

Prominent Nyingma proponents do not hesitate to assess esoteric theorems with tools they call "arguments" (*gtan tshigs*). Since the esoteric view is generally held to be superior to the sūtric by many Nyingma proponents, an assessment of that view through reason and arguments becomes more necessary for a proponent of the Early Translations than it would be in the context of a school in which it is held that the views of Madhyamaka and Mantra are essentially the same. A proponent of the latter will not see any real need to establish esoteric theorems such as purity, inseparability, etc. through reasoning, for the perfect view as presented in the Madhyamaka (or the Prāsaṅgika-Madhyamaka in particular) has already been perfectly assessed and established in its own context. Any additional assessment of that view in the esoteric context would be pointless. Rongzom's treatment of pure appearances implies, however, that pure appearances possess a distinct veridical value and this truth of purity must therefore, one way or the other, be ascertainable through reasoning. Purity, the Mahāyoga relative truth that is considered inseparable from the ultimate, has a decisive truth value for many Nyingma masters that remains unaccounted for in Sūtra. Thus, through the ages they have sought to underscore the central importance of purity through the use of arguments. The exegetical interplay among Nyingma scholars claiming the superiority of Mantra, and its consequences for the role of arguments, will be highlighted further in discussions below.

· 3 ·

Rongzom's View on Madhyamaka in Relation to Mantra

PROPONENTS of the Early Translations commonly assert a view of Mantra that supersedes in profundity the view of Sūtra, and they often support the validity of this view with the help of reasoning and logical arguments. Rongzom himself is a good illustration of this, as he argues for the superiority of the Mantra view and proposes the application of dialectical tools even on the esoteric level. When Rongzom states that the view of Mantra supersedes the Madhyamaka view it is necessary to understand what type of Madhyamaka he is referring to. We will now examine Rongzom's critique of Madhyamaka and how it illuminates his view of Mantra. We will also explore how this critique may have influenced Mipham, who considers Rongzom an important source of his Madhyamaka presentation.

A hermeneutical link can be demonstrated between Rongzom's critique of Madhyamaka and his promotion of the notion of purity on the esoteric level. Purity is a central theme in the esoteric tradition and, as we have seen, the view of Mantra is often distinguished from that of Sūtra with regard to purity or divinities. In examining Rongzom's view and critique of the Madhyamaka, insights can emerge about his view of Tantra and purity. Specifically, we shall examine

Rongzom's reservations regarding the Madhyamaka principles of relative truth and his opposition to a separation of the two truths.

Although Rongzom is often regarded as an apologist for the Nyingma tradition,[105] it is useful to investigate the extent to which his Madhyamaka discussion is apologetic in nature. Was it an attempt to thwart polemical attacks against the Dzogchen teachings? Here it will be argued that Rongzom should not be considered a source for the attempts of subsequent scholars to harmonize or minimize discrepancies between Mantrayāna/Dzogchen and the dialectical approach of Madhyamaka.[106] Although Rongzom was not against applying methodologies of the dialectical vehicle to establish the validity of Mantra, he clearly abstained from minimizing discrepancies between the views of Madhyamaka and Tantra. In this context, it will also be argued that Rongzom's Madhyamaka exegesis concerns what Mipham, his self-proclaimed follower, would have identified as Svātantrika and it is against this strand of Madhyamaka that Rongzom directs his critique. Although Rongzom never proposes a Madhyamaka view that resembles Mipham's later Prāsaṅgika interpretation in his extant writings, Mipham seems to assume that Rongzom was aware of both Prāsaṅgika and Svātantrika traditions, and he claims to base his own Madhyamaka philosophy on Rongzom's exegesis.[107] Chapter 3 will include reflections on this apparent paradox and offer some suggestions as to why Nyingma thinkers gradually came to consider the Prāsaṅgika Madhyamaka (*dbu ma thal 'gyur ba*) philosophy to be the paramount expression of the dialectical vehicle.

3.1 Rongzom's Madhyamaka

While the Madhyamaka was not necessarily considered the perfect expression of Buddhist philosophy in India,[108] Tibetan scholars, especially during the later dissemination of Buddhism, enthusiastically embraced the teachings of Madhyamaka as their philosophy *par excellence*. Over the years, Tibet became a hotbed for debates about which school presented the most authentic and profound Madhyamaka view. In this quest to determine the highest dialectical view, the school termed *Prāsaṅgika (*thal 'gyur ba*) emerged as the clear winner over its rival, the *Svātantrika (*rang rgyud pa*). Although the terms Svātantrika and Prāsaṅgika are most likely indigenous Tibetan creations,[109] their philosophical roots go back to the treatises of Buddhapālita, Candrakīrti, Bhāvaviveka, Śāntarakṣita, Kamalaśīla, et alii. Primarily, Candrakīrti's perspective on Madhyamaka became viewed as Prāsaṅgika, while that of masters such as Bhāvaviveka and Śāntarakṣita became known as Svātantrika. While the terms might seem to refer to rather self-evident philosophical viewpoints, Tibetan interpretations differ vastly in the way that they identify Prāsaṅgika and Svātantrika.[110]

No extensive exegesis on Madhyamaka by Rongzom remains extant. Yet we can find numerous compositions in which Rongzom contrasts the view of Madhyamaka with that of Tantra. For instance, in the *Memorandum on Views* Rongzom remarks, when elucidating the view of Mantrayāna, "The assertion that ultimately there is no birth and no cessation is the same as in Madhyamaka and that relatively the skandhas, dhātus, and āyatanas are mere illusion also concords. [But] in particular, it is a distinguishing feature [of the view of Mantrayāna] that it regards even the characteristics of illusion as the characteristics of complete divine purity, and also that it sees the two truths as inseparable."[111]

Rongzom continues to point out that there are numerous other inconsistencies between Sūtra and Mantra, such as Mantra being the object of experience only of those with keen faculties, those who master skillful means, those who have great compassion, etc.

Within the relative perspective, the difference between Sūtra and Mantra seems clear in that the latter regards illusion not merely as illusion but as divine purity. This appears to be a unique trait of the tantras. However, Rongzom initially asserts that the ultimate in both Sūtra and Mantra is the absence of birth and cessation—a description resonant with the "figurative," or "categorized," ultimate (*rnam grangs pa'i don dam, *paryāyaparamārtha*), which, according to Mipham, is emphasized by the Svātantrika (*Svātantrika, rang rgyud*).[112] Let us examine whether Rongzom's view of the ultimate truth of Madhyamaka could be equated to Mipham's description of the figurative ultimate. Mipham generally explains the figurative ultimate as a mere negation of the extreme of existence (*yod mtha'*), while the "nonfigurative," or "uncategorized," ultimate (*rnam grangs ma yin pa'i don dam, *aparyāyaparamārtha*) transcends the fourfold ontological extremes (*catuṣkoṭi*), i.e., existence, nonexistence, both, and neither.[113] In his *Commentary to the Garland of Views as Oral Instructions,* Rongzom defines these two divisions of the ultimate, speaking of the figurative ultimate and the "ultimate beyond mental constructs" (*spros pa dang bral ba'i don dam*), in the following way: "The figurative ultimate is the object of a mind in which mental constructs have been partially severed, and partially not severed. It is the purport of the terms that demonstrate the classifications of the ultimate, such as the eighteen [types] of emptiness. The ultimate beyond mental constructs is the nature of the complete pacification of all mental constructs."[114]

In his compositions, Rongzom repeatedly explains the ultimate Madhyamaka view as being free from mental contructs (*niṣprapañca*). This excludes the possibility of the ultimate being, in the Madhyamaka context, what Mipham calls "a mere existential negation" (*med dgag tsam*).[115] However, Rongzom's classifications of Madhyamaka schools differ from those applied by later scholars.

One might likewise anticipate that his view of the two truths as propagated by the Madhyamaka school also would diverge from later interpretations. Rongzom divides the Madhyamaka in the following way: "Although [the Mādhyamikas] concord in their view of the ultimate, [the school] is, with respect to [its view] regarding the relative [truth], divided into the Sautrāntika-Madhyamaka and the Yogācāra-Madhyamaka."[116]

Rongzom states that the Yogācāra-Madhyamaka school is superior to the Sautrāntika-Madhyamaka.[117] As scholars have already pointed out, Rongzom's extant writings make no mention of the Prāsaṅgika or its chief representative, Candrakīrti.[118] Patsab Nyima Drag (Spa tshab nyi ma grags) (1055-1145?), a contemporary of Rongzom, provided the basis for the Madhyamaka interpretations that became known as Prāsaṅgika with his translations of Candrakīrti's works.[119] Hence, the Svātantrika/Prāsaṅgika distinction, as a Tibetan doxographical principle, dates probably from the twelfth century.

Rongzom further divides the Madhyamaka into Sarvadharmāpratiṣṭhānavādins (*rab tu mi gnas pa*) and Māyopamādvayavādins (*sgyu ma rigs grub pa*).[120] Tsongkhapa and Khedrup both allude to ancient masters who identified the proponents of Sarvadharmāpratiṣṭhānavādins with the Prāsaṅgikas and the Māyopamādvayavādins with the Svātantrikas.[121] Keeping this in mind, as well as the fact that many of Rongzom's writings on the difference between Sarvadharmāpratiṣṭhānavādins and Māyopamādvayavādins listed in Rongpa Mepung's index (*tho yig*) appear to have been lost, it is problematic to rule out Rongzom's knowledge of Candrakīrti's Madhyamaka. Still, it is safe to argue that Rongzom's general explanations of the Madhyamaka differ in many ways from the Madhyamaka view propagated by Mipham centuries later. Although modern Nyingma scholars may depict Rongzom as a Prāsaṅgika-Mādhyamika, his general treatment of Madhyamaka indicates that the Madhyamaka with which he was concerned is exclusively of a type that Mipham would have identified as Svātantrika.

3.2 Rongzom's Reservations Regarding a Relative Truth Held to Be Distinct from the Ultimate

Rongzom usually divides the Mādhyamikas into Sautrāntika-Madhyamaka and Yogācāra-Madhyamaka, yet he also divides the school into Sarvadharmāpratiṣṭhānavādins and Māyopamādvayavādins. It is important to keep in mind that when Rongzom discusses Madhyamaka philosophy, his extant treatises usually do not indicate which Madhyamaka interpretation is in question. It is likewise noteworthy that he on no occasion refers to Candrakīrti, who is the paramount philosopher for the majority of later Tibetan Madhyamaka exponents.

Masters such as Bhāvaviveka and Śāntarakṣita, who are traditionally considered Svātantrika, adopted the epistemological tradition of Dignāga and Dharmakīrti to provide a reasoned account of convention, while Candrakīrti dismisses this foundational system of epistemology in his Madhyamaka approach.[122] Rongzom, while critical of Madhyamaka, does introduce Sūtra epistemology into his explanations, even in the Mantrayāna context. While he dismisses the Madhyamaka approach as imperfect and faulty, he at times employs methods that are characteristic of a Dharmakīrtian logician.

As a whole, Rongzom's extant corpus leads us to consider him primarily a tantrika or, perhaps, an advocate of the Great Perfection, who generally favored the suddenist approach to enlightenment and whose exegesis and critique of the sūtric philosophies primarily are carried out from an esoteric perspective. For instance, at the end of the first chapter of *Entering the Way of the Great Vehicle,* Rongzom relates how the Śrāvakas, the Yogācārins, and the Mādhyamikas refute themselves by asserting aspects of reality that either should be abandoned or differentiated from one another.[123] The Mādhyamikas defeat themselves by differentiating between the authentic and the inauthentic relative truths (*yang dag pa'i kun rdzob, log pa'i kun rdzob*). Rongzom points out that the Madhyamaka is not at fault here simply because the school's explanation conflicts with the way of unsurpassable Mantra. Rather, the Mādhyamikas "flaw themselves" (*rang la gnod pa*) because their presentation is inherently contradictory. Rongzom argues that they fail to see these flaws because they are attached to their philosophy.[124] He suggests that the different philosophies of Sūtrayāna defeat themselves through the inherent fallacies of their assertions, rather than through any conflict with the esoteric teachings. Rongzom's fondness for the tantric perspective quickly becomes apparent in his writings and on several occasions he targets the Madhyamaka's authentic relative truth (*yang dag pa'i kun rdzob*) as a principle that obstructs a final understanding of the ultimate.

Some Tibetan Mādhyamikas[125] perceive a major discrepancy between the Svātantrika and Prāsaṅgika schools in terms of whether an ontological commitment on the conventional level is made. They criticize the Svātantrika school for applying the foundational system of Dharmakīrti to relative reality, thereby attributing true objectivity to functional properties (*don byed nus pa'i dngos po*) of the authentic relative truth. For these thinkers, the Prāsaṅgika school does not reify relative phenomena in that manner. Instead of distinguishing between the functionality of objects themselves, they suggest an approach that decides on what is authentic or inauthentic simply based on subjective perceptions of the world. By avoiding a reification of the relative, the Prāsaṅgika becomes the superior view according to these scholars. Rongzom describes the Madhyamaka as a school that divides the relative into authentic and inauthentic based on the presence or absence of causal efficacy (*don byed nus pa, arthakriyāsamartha*) and, therefore, does not appear to consider Candrakīrti's approach of establishing the relative based on the perceiving subject rather than the object.

In this way, Rongzom expends a considerable amount of energy criticizing the Madhyamaka's two types of relative truth, defined with reference to objective efficacy or the lack of it. For instance, in *Entering the Way of the Great Vehicle,* he argues that both a vase and its reflection are equally able to perform a function. According to Rongzom, one must therefore accept that the division of the relative into authentic and false aspects based on efficacy is simply mistaken.[126] Likewise, he continues, the notion of functional things can be disproved even on the relative level: when analyzed into their constituent elements, all relative phenomena lose any appearance of being functional things, even on the very level of the relative. Thus, the qualities of the authentic and the false relative truth are entirely equal and neither of them possess any greater efficacy than the other. Rongzom argues vehemently against any attempt at ascribing a limited, i.e., not ultimately valid, sense of authenticity to certain aspects of the relative with the help of pointed anecdotes:

> [Trying to] establish [an authentic relative truth] is similar to grabbing onto a plant that is rotten from its root while one is being carried away by a river. It may be argued, "We do not assert any probandum on the ultimate level, and so mere relative [truth] is delightful to behold [only] so long as it is not investigated. If, however, it is investigated, it cannot withstand the load of

> reasoning and thus [the relevance of the authentic relative truth] is not contradicted by its being invalidated by reasoning."
>
> Well, [are you then saying] that mere establishment on the relative level does not require reasoning? If so, when you say that although they are similar in being appearances, the authentic and the inauthentic [relative truth] are posited and distinguished with reference to whether or not there is a presence of efficacy, is this then not reasoning? Whether established in reality or established merely on a temporary level, if something cannot even withstand the load of reasoning that pertains to its own specific level of existence, then how could that be said to exist even as mere convention! For instance, we may already have established that an elephant [which is supposed to] conquer the army of the enemy cannot bear the load of being steered by [the mahout's] hammer while carrying soldiers on its back. But if a cow [that is supposed to] simply plough the fields cannot carry the mere load of being steered by a bridle while carrying a yoke, then how can we establish even the mere conventions of it performing the function of ploughing fields? How will [that cow] be any different from goats?[127]

Once it has been established that not only can nothing remain as it appears in the face of ultimate investigation (as illustrated by the example of the elephant), we must also understand that things cannot retain their apparent status even on a relative level when submitted to analysis (as indicated by the example of the dysfunctional cow). Having understood this much, how could one assert a division of relative phenomena based on causal efficacy? The functional and the nonfunctional will have become indistinguishable and elephants, cows, and goats will be equally mere appearances. Rongzom concludes, "How could this [reference to apparently efficacious relative phenomena] make the label 'authentic relative' applicable, and how is this view different from that of an ordinary mundane individual? To hold such a view that isolates [the relative from the ultimate] is a cause for amazement!"[128]

To underscore the fallacy of a view that isolates the two truths from each other, Rongzom relates the story of a king whose desire was insatiable, and who was not satisfied even when coming to share the throne of the gods with Indra. He therefore fell from heaven down to earth, back into the realm of men, and only then discovered what he had lost. Struck by despair, he died of grief, destroyed by his own greedy desire. Rongzom uses this insatiable craving to illustrate the detrimental consequences of believing in an authentic relative truth: "If, since all phenomena are ultimately pacified beyond all mental constructs, one sees no probandum whatsoever to be proven, and yet at the same time still perceives certain characteristics of an authentic relative reality that contains substantial properties to be abandoned or accepted, that is an extremely inappropriate apprehension, and a cause for amazement."[129]

Rongzom proceeds to establish the equality of all perceptions through the well-known example of a rope perceived as a snake. One may first perceive the rope to be a snake and later come to see it as a rope. Yet the rope can also be understood to consist of parts, which in themselves again have parts, and so on *ad infinitum*. An analysis of what was originally perceived as a snake thus ends up as an understanding of emptiness. However, Rongzom points out, even the subtle emptiness of the particles in the rope is in fact only established with reference to entities. And since entities themselves are not established, emptiness becomes equally unestablished. Thus, he exclaims, "When one realizes that there is no property of a probandum whatsoever, then all is at the same level of nonexistence."[130]

The Prāsaṅgikas are generally thought to operate primarily through prāsaṅga, a *reductio* type of argument, as the means for arriving at an insight into emptiness. Thus, no commonly accepted subject is required as a basis for debate. Instead, the opponent's assertion is simply propelled *ad absurdum* by exposing its inherent inconsistencies, without the formulation of an antithesis on behalf of the Prāsaṅgika himself. When Rongzom argues against the possibility of a probandum being established, such statements, like his arguments against the authentic relative, resonate with a Prāsaṅgika approach that, apart from revealing the flaws of the opponent's assertion, refrains from making any claims on its own. Rongzom uses the same approach in the concise *Black Snake Discourse,* when he replies to an opponent (*pūrvapakṣa*) who wants to know what Rongzom is out to prove: "Apart from merely annulling your wicked views, we do not prove anything. Although conventionally this may be called the view of great equality, there is not the slightest concept of view."[131] While some of these passages may sound similar to the approach that Mipham explains as Prāsaṅgika, we must keep in mind that Rongzom is not explaining Madhyamaka, but criticizing it.

We have seen Rongzom arguing against a separation of the relative truth into two categories, one less unreal than the other. According to Rongzom, the inseparability of the two truths is a factor that distinguishes the view of Tantra from that of Madhyamaka. Rongzom explains in *Entering the Way of the Great Vehicle*: "The Mādhyamikas assert that all phenomena are without *svabhāva* . . . but since they do not abandon the concept of two truths, their view does not qualify as nondual."[132]

Throughout Rongzom's writings, we find ample evidence that for him a separation of the two truths, in the sense of conceptually isolating them from each other and ascribing to them each their own ontological status, is an error in the extreme. This also resonates with Mipham's Prāsaṅgika presentation.[133] In *Entering the Way of the Great Vehicle,* Rongzom says, "If one asserts that there is something to be authentically established, then all the particularities of the relative—however many there are—are likewise suited to be established. If, [however], one does not assert that there is anything to be established authentically, then all the particularities of the relative will be on the same level [of nonestablishment]."[134]

Thus Rongzom argues that both levels of truth, the relative and the ultimate, are equally *svabhāva*-less. He once more points out the futility and absurdity of considering everything to be ultimately unborn and yet continue to divide the relative into the dualism of authentic and false, thereby objectifying relative phenomena by perceiving them as entities that are to be accepted or rejected.

In the *Black Snake Discourse,*[135] Rongzom explains the differing approaches found within the Buddhist vehicles through the example of a black snake's reflection appearing in water. This discussion illustrates well Rongzom's critique of the Madhyamaka for failing to recognize the indivisibility of the two truths. Rongzom argues that the Mādhyamikas claim that, although in reality the snake's reflection is not substantially established and thus a mere illusion, it can nevertheless perform a relative function. Therefore, a Mādhyamika will only dare to approach the snake's reflection if he possesses a remedy or skillful means that can be applied against the illusory snake. In this way, Rongzom argues that, among the four types of existence (*yod pa, bhāva*),[136] the Mādhyamikas do not accept ultimate existence (*don dam par yod pa*), yet they do believe in relative existence (*kun rdzob tu yod pa*) and imputed existence (*btags su yod pa*). Rongzom, furthermore, explains that the view of the inseparability of the two truths begins to dawn with the tantras, yet it is only fully perfected in the Great Perfection. When an imaginary opponent inquires why the Madhyamaka does not set forth such a view of inseparability, Rongzom states that as long as one believes both truths to be true, one will never succeed in discarding the dualistic mindset. One could propose that ultimately the two truths are inseparable without giving up the idea that illusory phenomena exist on the relative level. Thus, even when attempting to establish *dharmatā* as nondual, one would still retain a dualistic perspective. The person who falls into this trap, Rongzom continues, might argue that what exists by way of imputation is *ultimately* free from mental constructs and therefore similar to illusion, yet he will not assert the same on the relative level, for he cannot accept that phenomena should lack substantial efficacy even conventionally. Thus, even while examining the characteristics of substantial existence and concluding that indeed such existence is unestablished, one will still not have mentally discarded the two ontological modes. Rongzom illustrates his point by referring to appearances (*snang ba*): as long as one assumes that there is an appearance that can be taken as the subject (*chos can, dharmin*) or used as an illustration (*mtshan gzhi, dṛṣṭānta*) in argument, and as long as one considers this property or illustration to be free from mental constructs (*spros bral, niṣprapañca*) and thus mere illusion, one still conceptualizes the characteristics of appearances. Therefore, the view of great equality remains yet to be accomplished, for by identifying a particular appearance and then concluding that this indeed is beyond mental constructs, the appearance aspect (*snang ba'i cha*) and the empty aspect (*stong pa'i cha*) become temporarily separated.

These explanations on the Mādhyamikas' lack of realization of the inseparability of the two truths are very telling, for they specify that appearances' aspect and their empty nature must be seen as inseparable for the view to qualify as great equality. Thus any objectification of the relative truth that specifies "authentic" (*yang dag*) relative principles would separate the two truths and prevent one from the sudden, full, and direct realization of the actual nature.

The view of equality is also explained as equality inseparable from purity. Let us consider a statement from Rongzom's commentary to the *Garland of Views as Oral Instructions*: "The Mādhyamikas are attached to the relative truth as being the experiential domain of impure characteristics."[137] Here Rongzom not only objects to the Madhyamaka belief in an authentic relative truth and its view of the two truths as separate identities, but also to the view of the relative as impurity. This underscores Rongzom's tantric perspective and his commitment to purity. Rongzom draws the dividing lines between Sūtra and Mantra based on a) whether relative truth is reified as distinct from the ultimate, as in the case of Madhyamaka, and b) whether, on the relative level, appearances are perceived as purity (Mantra) or impurity (Sūtra). Thus, for Rongzom, there is a clear connection between objectification of the relative and the view of impurity. For a tantrika like Rongzom, the Madhyamaka separation of ultimate and relative truths and the ensuing division of the relative into authentic and inauthentic aspects disparage the central esoteric notions of unity, equality, and purity. By setting forth an authentic relative and ascribing it a more genuine mode of existence than what is dismissed as the mistaken relative, one is blinded to the ultimate truth of great equality. Moreover, this equality is not realized, as the Mādhyamikas would have it, by a negation of relative phenomena. The ultimate equality, the nature of all phenomena, is inseparable from relative appearances, the appearances of great purity. In conclusion, according to Rongzom's tantric perspective, appearances are by nature pure and therefore need not be negated. As there is nothing to discard within their purity, everything remains as great equality. If phenomena were not universally pure, they could not be equal, and unless everything is absolutely equal, one cannot establish the truth of purity.

3.3 Rongzom's Influence on Mipham's Madhyamaka

Present-day scholars of the Nyingma school often portray Rongzom as a proponent of Prāsaṅgika-Madhyamaka and see Mipham as a follower of Rongzom's Prāsaṅgika. We shall now examine Mipham's interpretation of Madhyamaka, especially his promotion of the "unity of appearance and emptiness" (*snang stong zung 'jug*) and compare this with Rongzom's view.

We have noted that the Madhyamaka, in Rongzom's view, does not realize the inseparability of the two truths. This position, however, contradicts Mipham's common assertion that the unity of the two truths (*bden gnyis zung 'jug*) is the hallmark of the Prāsaṅgika's realization.[138] This difference of opinion is not surprising, as Rongzom may not have been aware of Candrakīrti and what Mipham interprets as his characteristic transcendence of the two-truths dichotomy. One might therefore take Rongzom's criticism of Madhyamaka philosophy as an indication that he only had knowledge of Yogācāra-Madhyamaka and Sautrāntika-Madhyamaka. Yet Mipham often claims to rely on Rongzom as a source for his Madhyamaka presentation. In the *Speech of Delight*, Mipham's foremost Madhyamaka treatise, he lists both Rongzom and Longchen Rabjam as central sources of reference and inspiration for his exegesis of Svātantrika and Prāsaṅgika-Madhyamaka.[139] The commentator on the *Beacon of Certainty*, Troshul Jamdor,[140] remarks, "Whenever Mipham Rinpoche ('Jam mgon bla ma) spoke of the Prāsaṅgika system or the difference between Prāsaṅgika and Svātantrika, he always based himself on Rongzom Paṇḍita and Longchen Rabjam."[141]

How is it that Mipham bases his Prāsaṅgika explanation on Rongzom when Rongzom never uses the term Prāsaṅgika nor mentions the name of the school's primary exponent, Candrakīrti? Mipham believes Candrakīrti's approach to be suddenist (*cig car*) in nature; an approach where the negation need not be specified as applying only to the ultimate level of things, and where the four extremes of the tetralemma (*catuṣkoṭi*) are eliminated simultaneously. By not crediting the relative truth with any sense of objectivity, the division into two levels of truth falls away and their unity (*zung 'jug*), or inseparability, is realized. From the very outset a capable follower of the Prāsaṅgika can, Mipham believes, find access to freedom from all mental constructs. The Prāsaṅgika, for Mipham, is therefore similar to the Great Perfection, which proclaims that because phenomena are pure or perfect since the very beginning, they require no negation or purification.[142]

While Mipham advocated this unity as the crucial and indispensable realization of the Madhyamaka, Rongzom appears never to have suggested that the Madhyamaka view could be described as the unity of appearance and emptiness (*snang stong zung 'jug*). Moreover, the term "unity of appearance and emptiness" with which Mipham describes the relationship between appearance and emptiness for the Prāsaṅgika was most likely originally used only in the esoteric context. The classical Indian Madhyamaka authors, to my knowledge, never explicitly speak of appearance and emptiness as being a unity (*zung 'jug*). For Mipham, however, this principle implies the equal veridical value of the two truths of appearance and emptiness in the Madhyamaka context.[143] In taking this position, Mipham comes close to the assertions of an inseparability of the two truths that Rongzom and other Nyingma philosophers posit in the Mantrayāna context.

We have seen how Rongzom argues against any separation of the two truths and the ensuing conceptual distinctions between appearance (*snang ba*) and freedom from mental constructs (*spros bral*). We have likewise noted in chapter 2 that Mipham only equates Madhyamaka with the Great Perfection when appearances and emptiness are viewed simultaneously rather than sequentially. While Rongzom criticizes Madhyamaka from an esoteric perspective, Mipham defines Madhyamaka in a way that avoids the very faults that Rongzom objects to. While the term "appearance" (*snang ba*) in the Madhyamaka context includes all types of appearances, both pure and impure, the view of the higher tantras precludes anything impure.[144] Thus Mipham's Madhyamaka can only avoid Rongzom's critique this far. However, in the *Beacon of Certainty,* Mipham implies that the Madhyamaka view of the unity, or inseparability, of the two truths *qua* appearance and emptiness does involve a sense of purity, for appearances are primordially pure in being equally empty and apparent. In the same text, Mipham even suggests a strong link between Rongzom and Candrakīrti:

> The glorious Candrakīrti in India
> And Rongzom Chözang in Tibet
> With one voice and one intent
> Established the great emptiness of primordial purity.
> Because these phenomena are primordially pure,
> Or because they are primordially without intrinsic nature,
> They are not born in either of the two truths.[145]

It is intriguing that Rongzom would have established emptiness and primordial purity (*ka dag*) in unison with Candrakīrti, whose texts he never refers to and whom he may not have known. However, Rongzom objected vehemently to any objectively established reality and dismissed any sense of truth that would involve impure characteristics. He professed a view in which all phenomena are nothing but emptiness from the very outset. According to Mipham's exegesis, Candrakīrti likewise advocates a suddenist path that transcends conceptual extremes and constructs without ascribing any privileged status to certain aspects of the relative truth.[146] Both Rongzom and Candrakīrti were proponents of the *svabhāva*-lessness of both truths.[147] From this perspective, they agree in their way of establishing emptiness. But how can Candrakīrti be said to establish primordial purity, a Dzogchen term that only appears in later Tibetan literature? In the works of Longchen Rabjam, the term "primordial purity" (*ka dag*) serves as a Great Perfection synonym for emptiness,[148] signifying the lack of establishment of all phenomena from the very beginning. In this light, Mipham's parallel between the views of Candrakīrti and Rongzom appears more tenable. Furthermore, Candrakīrti resists the tendency to objectify the relative by dividing it into authentic and false properties, just as Rongzom attacks such classifications as belying the equally empty nature of all phenomena. While "primordial purity" (*ka dag*) in Longchen Rabjam's works differs from the term "purity" (*dag pa*) in the Mahāyoga context, Rongzom still establishes purity (*dag pa*) with reference to emptiness in *Establishing Appearances as Divine*[149] and he argues that the two Mahāyoga truths of purity and equality necessarily entail each other, given their inseparability. According to central Nyingma proponents, purity in the esoteric teachings is in this sense closely related to the absence of any objective relative truth. Regardless of how unreal it may ultimately be, any authentic relative truth would defy the pervasive nature of emptiness/equality. If the purity of appearances taught in Mantra establishes appearances as the natural expression of emptiness, an emptiness that transcends probanda and neganda even on the relative level, Mipham's identification of a philosophical kinship between Candrakīrti and Rongzom becomes more feasible than what first appears.

The separation of the two truths and the objectification of relative truth are considered untenable both by Rongzom and Mipham.[150] However, when Mipham propounds the Prāsaṅgika-Madhyamaka he operates within a sūtric perspective,[151] whereas Rongzom's criticism of the Madhyamaka is tantra-based. Mipham's Prāsaṅgika exegesis and Rongzom's Madhyamaka criticism are still often intriguingly close. Rongzom's central objections to the separation of two types of relative truth, based on defining relative truth as what is causally efficacious, therefore turn entirely towards a philosophy that Mipham would classify, and criticize, as Svātantrika. Thus while Rongzom criticizes Madhyamaka for its lack of recognition of the inseparability of the two truths, and Mipham extols the Madhyamaka for its perfect acknowledgment of that very inseparability, the implications of their words seem to be the same. Mipham, who claims to be strongly influenced by Rongzom in his Madhyamaka exegesis, speaks of the Prāsaṅgika-Madhyamaka as a school whose final insight is the unity of the two truths. Mipham considers Candrakīrti a philosopher who, reluctant to separate the two truths, avoids "qualifying the object of refutation with the term 'ultimate'" (*dgag bya la don dam pa'i khyad par sbyar ba*),[152] hence denying *svabhāva* on both levels of truth. Mipham takes Rongzom's esoteric critique of Madhyamaka into account here, for he presents the Prāsaṅgika approach in a way that concurs with Mantra's proclamation of the two truths as inseparable. In Mipham's Prāsaṅgika exegesis, the two truths of appearance and emptiness bear equal value and entail each other, and it is in this light that Mipham can be said to have relied on Rongzom in his Madhyamaka explanations. Yet, in establishing the Madhyamaka as a flawless approach, or proposing a link between the Madhyamaka and the inner tantras, he did not follow Rongzom, for such exegetical moves are found nowhere in Rongzom's extant works. We can conclude that

Mipham considered Rongzom's critique to be of a Madhyamaka that, seen from Rongzom's esoteric perspective, is an imperfect system that creates an unnatural conflict between the two truths, and thus, we may say, Mipham sought to formulate a Prāsaṅgika that would deflect precisely that criticism. Mipham's all-important use of the term "unity" (*zung 'jug*) is a clear indicator of a deep tantric influence underlying his presentation of Madhyamaka.

We could investigate other issues to evaluate the influence of Rongzom's Madhyamaka critique on subsequent Nyingma thought. For instance, in concluding this discussion let us again notice how, for Mipham, the notion of an objective reality, even on the merely relative level, is a hindrance to the suddenist path because it provisionally divides the two truths and excludes the aspect of appearance or purity from that of emptiness. The emphasis on a suddenist path is a hallmark of the Ancient Translation School, and this feature is clearly present in both Mipham's and Rongzom's Madhyamaka treatment. When Mipham links Candrakīrti and Rongzom (and, by extension, himself), he underscores the importance of the suddenist approach. His discourse is thus aligned with the view of Dzogchen, which the Nyingma tradition considers to be the pinnacle of all teaching, transcending a gradual path. Considering that the Nyingma school was often criticized for being similar to Chinese Ch'an Buddhism,[153] Mipham's explicit alignment of Rongzom with Candrakīrti might also have been an attempt to thwart such criticism. Demonstrating a predilection for the suddenist path even in the works of Candrakīrti—who in Tibet had become almost universally celebrated as a paramount philosopher among the masters of India—would in many ways have automatically established the general validity of the suddenist approach.

3.4 Concluding Reflections

If we were to establish Rongzom's personal view by reversing all the philosophical features that he discards as imperfect characteristics of Madhyamaka, terms such as "absence of objectivity," "purity," "equality," and "inseparability of the two truths" would stand out. For Rongzom, the view of Mantra transcends impurity, divisions within the relative truth, and ontological polarizations of the two truths. The hermeneutical link to purity in Rongzom's critique of Madhyamaka emerges particularly in his vehement criticism of the objectification of the relative truth. According to Rongzom, if a distinct veridical status were ascribed to an authentic relative (*yang dag pa'i kun rdzob*) with reference to its ability, albeit only relative, to function within the realm of karma and *kleśas,* it would clearly denigrate the principle of purity, the relative truth of the Mahāyoga. By holding such an objectified authentic relative to be true on its own level, yet ultimately false, the two truths could indeed not be inseparable. They would be alienated from each other in a way that, for Rongzom the tantrika, goes starkly against the abiding condition (*gnas lugs*), in which purity and equality are inseparable.[154]

In chapter 2, we saw that Sapaṇ and Tsongkhapa both consider the views of Tantra and Madhyamaka equivalent. In this way, they legitimize the esoteric teachings by grounding them within the exoteric. Rongzom, however, consistently considers the Madhyamaka view less profound than the tantric. Given the explicit nature of his critique, we have no reason to believe that Rongzom saw any purpose in using Madhyamaka teachings as an apologetic means for establishing the validity of Mantra. Still, he displays a general fondness for the application of Buddhist epistemological tools to validate both Mantrayāna and Dzogchen. Did Rongzom refrain from proposing a closer relationship between Madhyamaka and the inner tantras simply because he was unaware of Candrakīrti's Madhyamaka and the Prāsaṅgika refinements that Longchen Rabjam and Mipham would later extol? The answer will remain elusive in the absence of decisive historical evidence regarding the origins of Prāsaṅgika interpretations in Tibet; yet taking into account Rongzom's critique of the objective authentic relative and the, for him, thereby ensuing division between the two truths, we can speculate that he would have felt more at ease with Candrakīrti's subject-based classifications of the two relative truths.

Both Mipham and Rongzom advocate an esoteric view that supersedes the view of Madhyamaka (Rongzom more consistently than Mipham). Still, they do not dismiss the methods employed in the dialectical vehicle, but bring them right into the Mantra context. It is characteristic of many proponents of the Early Translations, including Rongzom and Mipham, that philosophical views are seen as increasingly profound to the degree that they establish the intrinsic unity of the two truths. When Rongzom discusses Madhyamaka, he operates from an esoteric perspective and rarely clarifies in his critique which, or even whether, a particular Madhyamaka subschool is under examination. However, considering his emphasis on a Madhyamaka division into two relative truths based on causal efficacy, and his repeated critique of the school's separation of the two truths, the Madhyamaka to which Rongzom objects seems concordant with Mipham's Svātantrika description.

Finally, as we close the treatment of Rongzom's Madhyamaka and its implications for the Nyingma school, we may finally consider whether Tsongkhapa's successful propagation of Prāsaṅgika as the philosophy *par excellence* forced other Tibetan schools to follow suit in setting forth the Prāsaṅgika as the paramount view of the dialectical vehicle, even if their interpretation of Madhyamaka differed vastly from Tsongkhapa's.[155] While this may be a compelling idea, it is likely that there were other reasons why the Nyingma school adopted Candrakīrti's Madhyamaka as the favored view in the dialectical context. Rongzom's appraisal insists that a separation of the two truths that attributes objectivity to the relative is a severe mistake, and therefore not in tune with either the inner tantras in general or the Dzogchen view in particular. Given Candrakīrti's critique of attempts to reify the relative and his reluctance to consider certain parts of the relative experience—i.e., the authentic relative (*yang dag pa'i kun rdzob*)—as more authentic than others, many Nyingma philosophers might indeed have seen his Madhyamaka as genuinely closer to the Dzogchen teachings than any other Sūtrayāna approach. Rongzom criticizes the Madhyamaka for advocating a dualism between the two truths and thus creating a sense of objective reality regarding the relative truth. In this we find a precursor to Mipham's later propagation of a Prāsaṅgika interpretation that transcends such flaws. Thus, while Rongzom primarily criticized the Madhyamaka view as imperfect, his critique might have inspired an enthusiastic adoption of Prāsaṅgika-Madhyamaka in the Nyingma school.

· 4 ·

Rongzom's Four Principles of Reasoning as Means for Establishing Purity

By now we have seen that Rongzom regards the views of the Sūtrayāna as inferior to those of Mantra, and he underscores his commitment to the purity of all phenomena by criticizing the Madhyamaka objectification of the authentic relative truth. We will now investigate Rongzom's perspective on reasoning *per se* and survey his use of the four principles of reasoning through which he seeks to establish a superior ontological status of purity. These attempts by Rongzom to prove purity through reasoning may have had an important impact on the later Nyingma master Mipham and we will look into Rongzom's possible influence on Mipham's evaluation of pure appearances.

Valuing purity as a crucial exegetical element, Rongzom is keen on presenting this principle in a way that is sound and rational. In *Establishing Appearances as Divine,* Rongzom uses four principles of reasoning (*rigs pa bzhi, yukti-catuṣṭayam*) to establish purity. Rongzom refuses, as do later representatives of the Nyingma school, to confine the application of rational tools to the Sūtra level only and instead sets out to prove the validity of esoteric theorems by means of these general mahāyānic principles. The four principles of reasoning are thus assigned a very central role in *Establishing*

Appearances as Divine. Rongzom also treats them in detail in *Entering the Way of the Great Vehicle.* These two texts will provide our primary sources for the discussion of Rongzom's application of the four principles.

To begin, we will briefly investigate the four principles in general and the meaning of the term "reasoning" (*rigs pa*). We shall also examine what role reasoning *per se* might play in Rongzom's philosophical project. The following subchapters will present an overview of each of these four principles of reasoning.

Among the four reasonings, we shall focus on the reasoning of the intrinsic nature (*chos nyid kyi rigs pa*), as Rongzom's treatment of this reasoning appears somewhat unconventional. While focusing on Rongzom's own definitions and assessment, we shall also compare these with principles found mainly in three other sources: the *Saṁdhinirmocanasūtra*, *Abhidharmasamuccaya*, and the *Valid Means of Cognition*. Finally, in chapter 4.5 we shall briefly consider Rongzom's influence on Mipham's evaluation of purity. Rongzom's attempt to prove purity through the four reasonings in *Establishing Appearances as Divine* may have inspired Mipham to allocate a specific valid cognition for purity, and Mipham's treatment may reciprocally shed light on Rongzom's stance.

One may wonder which scriptures inspired Rongzom to establish purity by means of the four principles of reasoning (*rigs pa bzhi, yukti-catuṣṭayam*). The *Saṁdhinirmocanasūtra*, the earliest known source that employs the four principles of reasoning, certainly may have been an inspiration. Another source that may have played a role is Asaṅga's *Śrāvakabhūmi,* in which Asaṅga argues for the *im*pure nature of things using exactly these four principles.[156]

The four principles of reasoning are classically treated in Asaṅga's *Abhidharmasamuccaya* and Maitreya's *Mahāyānasūtrālaṃkāra,* and Rongzom no doubt was familiar with these texts. Furthermore, we might also notice the *Valid Means of Cognition,* attributed to Trisong Deutsen, as a possible source of inspiration for Rongzom with its elaborate treatment of the four principles.

To determine the status of the four reasonings in the Nyingma school, Mipham's well-known abhidharma treatise, the *Gateway to Knowledge,*[157] and his concise *Sword of Wisdom*[158] offer valuable insights. Mipham, however, arranges the four principles in a different sequence than the *Saṁdhinirmocanasūtra,* while Rongzom uses another sequence altogether. In both *Establishing Appearances as Divine* and *Entering the Way of the Great Vehicle,* Rongzom uses the same sequential arrangement, beginning with the principle of the intrinsic nature followed by the reasoning of efficacy, the reasoning of dependence, and finally the reasoning of valid proof. It appears that Rongzom has specific reasons for choosing a presentation of the four reasonings that differs from the canonical.

In a modern Nyingma textbook on Pramāṇa, *Steps to Valid Reasoning,*[159] Rongzom's explanations of the four principles are the ones most frequently cited, along with those of Mipham and Trisong Deutsen, and we shall examine this concise text to add a contemporary perspective.

Steps to Valid Reasoning quotes Rongzom's explanation of the general term "reasoning" (*rigs pa*) in the following way: "The term for 'reason' is *nyāya. Nyāya* also refers to 'nature' and 'way' and hence the nature of things, just as it is, is called 'reason.' Another term is *yukti,* which implies the possession of reason and hence reasoning."[160]

Mipham, in his *Gateway to Knowledge,* plays with the double connotation (subjective and objective) of the Tibetan term *rigs pa* when explaining its etymology: "Since this abidance of the nature of phenomena is appropriate and reasonable, it is called *rigs pa* ('reasoning'). To evaluate in accordance with [this nature] is [likewise] termed *rigs pa* ('reasoning')."[161]

Yoshimizu remarks on the term "reasoning" (*rigs pa, yukti*) as it appears in the *Saṁdhinirmocanasūtra, Śrāvakabhūmi,* and *Abhidharmasamuccaya,* that it "is assumed to mean an objective ground or principle which consists of the phenomenal world or facts and based on which one can explain originations and changes of phenomena as well as relations between things including logical relations."[162]

In *Steps to Valid Reasoning,* Rongzom is quoted: "Thus, the term 'reasoning' refers to both the object's exact way of abiding and to the mind that is in accord with that. Therefore, one must understand that it applies equally to the defining characteristics of the object and the mind [that cognizes] in accord with those."[163]

According to *Steps to Valid Reasoning,* these two aspects of reasoning, the objective and the subjective, are subdivided into the four principles of reasoning. In this way one arrives at eight different reasonings by reference to either object cognized or cognizing subject.[164] However, Rongzom's explanations of the four principles, as found in *Entering the Way of the Great Vehicle,* relate mostly to the perspective of an examining subject, without any sense of referring to an objective condition of that which is evaluated.

In studying Rongzom's treatment of reasoning, a certain ambiguity with regard to the status and value of reasoning itself becomes apparent. For instance, in *Establishing Appearances as Divine* Rongzom states:

> The conceptual mind that takes objects that appear in the experience of sentient beings as valid is since beginningless time deluded. It accepts or negates with reference to the way things appear to it. With such dialectics it is indeed not possible to establish the vast and profound meaning. But nevertheless, since the nature of phenomena is inconceivable, it is not the case that one

> cannot realize it by means of discriminating knowledge. It is thus not in any way a mistake if one, rather than that, is inclined to approach simply by faith. By regarding the scriptures and oral instructions as valid, one will then gain access through trust.[165]

Again, when explaining the final reasoning, the principle of valid proof, Rongzom downplays its value, presenting it merely as an expedient means: "For those of inferior capacity, reasoning itself is to be established first, so that they can evaluate the meaning, and proof must thus be made by means of a definite subject, probandum, example, and forward and reverse pervasion."[166]

In spite of Rongzom's attempts to establish the intrinsic nature (*chos nyid, dharmatā*) by way of reasoning, and his general appreciation for rationality, he also limits the role of reasoning in the discovery and ascertainment of reality. In the chapter of *Entering the Way of the Great Vehicle* where Rongzom argues that the Great Perfection cannot be invalidated through reasoning, he states that it is the treatises on logic (*rigs pa'i bstan bcos*) that establish and negate by means of the four principles of reasoning. Rongzom proceeds to argue that they do not actually ascertain anything but are mere constructions of establishment and negation. In this way, any veracity of the process is close to absent: "[People] may evaluate by means of the four principles, but what is observed [thereby] is merely one realist philosophy invalidating another. Moreover, as [the victorious] reasoning [upon investigation also] itself will be [seen to be] absurd, it will in the end be seen to be invalid."[167]

Rongzom presents a rather blunt and disillusioned assessment of the nature of reasoning: the four principles of reasoning cannot go beyond the purview of realism and, if relying on reasoning alone, one is certain to see one's conclusions invalidated. Why, then, does

Rongzom display such fondness for reasoning in general, and why does he bother with a detailed exposition of the nature of the four principles if reasoning in general, and the four principles in particular, are so obviously limited? Could it be that while Rongzom himself considers the scope and accuracy of reasoning strongly confined, he simply chose to go with the general flow of his time, a time when logic and epistemology were flourishing? Perhaps Rongzom chose to employ tools that were fashionable in his time primarily to provide credibility to his views and agenda and thus cater to an audience that was well versed in logic and epistemology. Considering the popularity of Buddhist epistemology and logic *à la* Dignāga and Dharmakīrti as part of monastic study and curricula, Rongzom could use his discussion of reasoning to engage with monastic scholasticism that may otherwise have been critical of lay tantrikas and their tradition. Whatever the case, throughout his writings Rongzom describes the narrow confines and dubious relevance of reasoning even as he enthusiastically applies the various principles of Buddhist reasoning to achieve his purposes, displaying a remarkable ambiguity with respect to the nature and validity of reasoning.

Let us now turn to an examination of each of the four principles of reasoning as they appear in *Establishing Appearances as Divine* and *Entering the Way of the Great Vehicle*. We will juxtapose Rongzom's explanations with definitions and remarks from other texts, especially the *Valid Means of Cognition, Abhidharmasamuccaya,* and *Saṁdhinirmocanasūtra.*

4.1 The Reasoning of Intrinsic Nature (*chos nyid kyi rigs pa, dharmatāyukti*)

The principle of intrinsic nature constitutes one of the most complex and elusive aspects of Buddhist reasoning. While the remaining three principles of reasoning base their conclusions on formal rational thought processes, the principle of intrinsic nature expresses surprisingly little "reason" (*rgyu mtshan, hetu*) and mostly presents bare statements rather than results arrived at through logical investigation. Let us nevertheless try to meet this enigmatic principle head on, with its challenge to the ordinary assumption that reasoning should necessarily involve reasons extrinsic to the very thing investigated.

Valid Means of Cognition proposes a brief definition of the principle of intrinsic nature: "What we call reasoning of the intrinsic nature is explained with reference to the nature of phenomena. It is what reveals the respective nature of phenomena, whether they are of relative or ultimate truth."[168]

Valid Means of Cognition continues its assessment of the reasoning of intrinsic nature by explaining that "the truth of all phenomena is also called the reasoning of the intrinsic nature" and then subsequently enumerates ten principles of truth: "The relative truth, the ultimate truth, the truth of characteristics, the truth of complete discernment, the truth of certain realization, the truth of entity, the truth of capability, the truth of the knowledge of exhaustion and nonarising, the truth of the knowledge of entering the path, and the truth of the origin of the wisdom of the Thus Gone Ones. Those are the ten truths."[169]

Here we shall not address these truths individually, but the reasoning of the intrinsic nature perhaps is better understood as a statement of veridical values with respect to phenomena rather than an explanation of such values by means of reasoning. While the other principles operate in a way that closely resembles our common expectation of reasoning, the reasoning of the intrinsic nature limits itself to a list of assertions regarding aspects or levels of truth. This particular functioning of the reasoning of *dharmatā* is later clarified by Rongzom as he describes its limitations and potential unfortunate consequences.

In *Entering the Way of the Great Vehicle,* Rongzom explains the reasoning of the intrinsic nature in a way similar to the sources cited above: "The reasoning of the intrinsic nature is to establish [the phenomenon] with respect to its essence."[170]

Moreover, when defining the "exclusions" (*sel ba*) which the four principles effectuate, Rongzom explains the exclusion particular to the principle of the intrinsic nature as the elimination of "doubts regarding the essence of things."[171] The *Abhidharmasamuccaya* defines the reasoning of *dharmatā* in the following way: "All phenomena abide since beginningless time by their own and general characteristics. This is known as the intrinsic nature."[172]

The *Saṁdhinirmocanasūtra*, probably the earliest text to explain this reasoning, states, "Whether the Tathāgata previously has appeared in the world, or whether he has not, the way the intrinsic nature abides and the way the basic space of phenomena abides is [itself] the reasoning of the intrinsic nature."[173]

While the definitions of *Entering the Way of the Great Vehicle* and the *Abhidharmasamuccaya* describe reasoning *qua* means for logical conclusions, the quote from the *Saṁdhinirmocanasūtra* does not present such a reasoning, but rather nature itself. The principle of the intrinsic nature is often employed by present-day commentators in a way that does not differ from the *Saṁdhinirmocanasūtra's* simple deferral to a natural condition of things. For instance, it is taught that fire is hot because heat is the nature of fire (i.e., the reasoning of the intrinsic nature) and that not even the Buddha would be able to explain this phenomenon further.

This assertion appears similar to the Buddhist depictions of the view held by the non-Buddhist school of the Cārvākas, who proclaim that the reason for any event (e.g., water falling or the sun rising) rests exclusively on the nature of things. Mipham, in his commentary to the *Madhyamakālaṃkāra*, describes how the Cārvākas illustrate this type of natural occurrence: "The examples of origination by the essential nature [employed by the Cārvākas] are the sun rising, water falling, the round pea, the sharp thorn, and so forth."[174]

Jamgon Kongtrul's explanations of the principle of the intrinsic nature appear strikingly similar to the views ascribed to the Cārvākas:

> It is the principle of reason that water falls downwards and not a principle of reason that it falls upwards. [The principle here considered] also includes generic properties (Tib. *chos spyi*; Skt. *sāmānyadharma*) and individuating characteristics (Tib. *rang gi mtshan nyid*; Skt. *svalakṣaṇa*), such as the sun's rising in the east, the solidity of earth, the wetness of water, the heat of fire, and the motility of air, as well as emptiness and absence of self. These, which are well known as thus abiding by their own natures from all eternity (*thog ma med pa'i dus nas*), are the principle of reality.[175]

When considered in its context, Jamgon Kongtrul's explanation of the Buddhist notion of the reasoning of *dharmatā* is in many regards dramatically different from the ideas of the materialist Cārvākas.[176] It is, nevertheless, tempting to draw certain parallels between the two, and this might have compelled Rongzom, in *Entering the Way of the Great Vehicle*, to warn against an excessive application of this principle of reasoning: "If proof by means of the reasoning of the intrinsic nature is applied in excess, all entities will not be annulled and in the end you will become a proponent of nature being the cause [of things]."[177] A few lines later,

Rongzom again cautions against pitfalls related to the reasoning of the intrinsic nature: "When proponents of entities [i.e., realists] prove entities, they mostly will do so through the reasoning of the intrinsic nature and with reference to direct perception. Hence, I shall explain the limits and consequences of this [reasoning]."[178]

Rongzom's skeptical treatment of the principle of the intrinsic nature contrasts with the views of Mipham and Jamgon Kongtrul.[179] In *Entering the Way of the Great Vehicle,* Rongzom describes[180] how perception (*'du shes, saṃjñā*) and feeling (*tshor ba, vedanā*) cannot clear away all stains of confusion (*'khrul pa*), exaggeration (*sgro*), and denigration (*skur*), whereas stainless knowledge (*shes rab dri ma med pa*) can. Stainless knowledge is of a twofold nature: discriminative knowledge (*so sor rtog pa'i shes rab*) and nonconceptual knowledge (*rnam par mi rtog pa'i shes rab*). Discriminative knowledge gradually dispels most confusion but not all unless "the main part of the intrinsic nature is annulled" (*cho nyid kyi dngos gzhi log pa*). However, actualizing the "annulment of *chos nyid*" is only possible by way of nonconceptual wisdom (*rnam par mi rtog pa'i ye shes*).[181] Rongzom concludes that any establishment through the reasoning of the intrinsic nature will necessarily be imperfect and, because it involves conceptual grasping at intrinsic nature, this reasoning can only partially dispel the stains of the mind. He explains some of the unfortunate consequences of this type of establishment:[182]

> If the [principle of the intrinsic nature is relied on] excessively, [the principle] becomes just like the Madhyamaka's authentic relative truth, where poison has an inherently lethal nature and medicine an inherently healing nature. If [those qualities] would be the intrinsic nature of entities, then also the ultimate existence of the mind and wis-

> dom in the Yogācāra would become the intrinsic nature, [the same would be the case with] the dualistic fixation of a Śrāvaka, and finally one would end up a proponent of nature being the [universal] cause. Thus, [this principle can] turn into the guardian of all realist views.[183]

In other words, if by deference to the intrinsic nature one accepts that phenomena are in themselves either good or bad, true or false, rejectable or acceptable then, no matter how sophisticated one's judgments may be, one's view will not be beyond that of a realist (*dngos por smra ba*). It once more becomes clear that Rongzom is no proponent of *svabhāvas.*[184]

Rongzom speaks of "annulling the intrinsic nature" (*chos nyid log pa/ldog pa*).[185] To Rongzom, such an "annulment" of the intrinsic nature appears to be a prerequisite for dissolving all realist views and perceptions. Given that intrinsic nature (*chos nyid, dharmatā*) is treated as a negandum in much the same way that independent nature (*rang bzhin, svabhāva*) is attacked in classical Madhyamaka texts, annulling the intrinsic nature simply comes down to establishing phenomena as devoid of independent nature (*svabhāva*). According to Rongzom, no independent or intrinsic nature can be rightly and reasonably demonstrated, neither on a relative nor on an ultimate level. Does the annulment and voidness of *dharmatā* then equal establishment of the "true nature" of all phenomena for Rongzom? Given his general displeasure with any potentially reifying commitments, it seems plausible that Rongzom would have objected to such an identification of the voidness of the intrinsic nature as being the true nature of things.

When Rongzom defines (with enigmatic terminology) the object (*yul*) and the limitations (*tshad*) of this principle of reasoning, he states:

> Whenever the main part of the intrinsic nature is stainless and not annulled, then this can appropriately be posited as the reasoning of the intrinsic nature . . . As for the main part of the intrinsic nature being stained, that would be for instance a sun crystal [used to produce fire by concentrating the sun's rays] being hot to the touch. An example of the main part being annulled would be when for the deer [known as] "that which cleanses itself in fire" the main part of fire's heat is annulled [i.e., when it is not burned although bathing in fire].[186]

Whatever the full implications of this passage might be, Rongzom makes it clear that he considers the reasoning of the intrinsic nature only a reasoning insofar as "the main part of the intrinsic nature is not annulled"—that is, only for as long as the object under examination displays qualities or characteristics that appear "natural" to it. So, we may surmise, when *dharmatā* is annulled, i.e., when natural properties are no longer determinable, reasoning no longer applies. In this way the possibility presents itself that Rongzom occasionally equates intrinsic nature with *svabhāva*, implying that the term "intrinsic nature" may differ from the actual, abiding way of phenomena and refer instead to a superimposition (*sgro skur, samāropa*) on par with the status of independent nature in the Madhyamaka context.[187] Perhaps for Rongzom the annihilation of *dharmatā* is necessary for a perception of the abiding condition (*gnas lugs*) of all things. In any case, Rongzom's approach to the reasoning of intrinsic nature can very well be classified as "anti-*svabhāva*."

In Mipham's concise *Sword of Wisdom* we come across an often-quoted statement that may shed light on the nature of the reasoning of the intrinsic nature:

> When having reached the end of reasoning within the
> intrinsic nature,
> No further reason is to be sought.[188]

According to Mipham, when the intrinsic nature has been reached, reasoning is no longer applicable. Rongzom puts it differently: when the intrinsic nature itself has been annulled, there is no more reasoning either. Mipham never talks about any need for the intrinsic nature itself to be annulled or reversed, while for Rongzom the reversal of the intrinsic nature is an important theme. Although the inapplicability of further reasoning beyond the intrinsic nature that Mipham proposes is at odds with Rongzom's explanations, it may nevertheless prove helpful for understanding why the reasoning of the intrinsic nature is classified as a reasoning although its presentation lacks the argumentation one would expect from reasoning. According to Mipham, one may come to an understanding of the relative intrinsic nature through the other three types of reasoning: dependency, efficacy, and valid proof. Yet having arrived at that intrinsic nature, no further reasoning is sought. Aside from becoming aware that this is simply the nature of phenomena, i.e., being brought face to face with the reasoning of the intrinsic nature, there is nothing left for the intellect to do or comprehend. Thus although this principle carries a sense of absence of further supportive evidence, yet within that there is a perfect acknowledgment of the bare facts.

In discussing Mipham's assessment of the principle of the intrinsic nature and his move to determine a conventional and ultimate aspect of this reasoning, Kapstein suggests:

> The conventional aspect of the principle of reality, taken
> metaphysically, would then amount to the principle that

> the reality of a thing is exhausted in its complete concept; and, taken epistemologically, it would amount to the assertion that a thing is known when one attributes to it some set of properties that constitute a complete definition of that very thing. The absolute aspect of the principle of reality would then be a negative thesis to the effect that the complete concept of a thing neither involves, nor entails, the intrinsic being of that thing. [189]

When comparing Mipham's view, as seen by Kapstein,[190] with Rongzom's, we observe that Rongzom, unlike Mipham, does not deem it necessary to split the intrinsic nature into a relative/ultimate dichotomy. Rongzom often argues strongly against any notion of a relative truth that retains a sense of establishment, however limited, despite its ultimately empty nature. In fact, in describing the reasoning of the intrinsic nature as necessarily incapable of annulling the idea of the intrinsic nature itself, Rongzom denies any ultimate validity of this reasoning.

Rongzom's explanations of the reasoning of the intrinsic nature are, we can conclude, often unconventional and deserve more scholarly attention. In *Entering the Way of the Great Vehicle* and *Establishing Appearances as Divine*, Rongzom deviates from the customary order of the four principles of reasoning as he places the reasoning of the intrinsic nature, usually the last in the set, as the first. Speculating about his motives for this puzzling sequence might enrich our understanding of his underlying point of view. The original sequence set forth in the *Saṁdhinirmocanasūtra* may have a propaedeutic value, leading the student gradually to an understanding of the intrinsic nature. Why then does Rongzom begin his explanation with the reasoning of the intrinsic nature—the reasoning that displays the least argumentative reason and evidence? From *Establishing Appearances as Divine,* it would appear that Rongzom seeks to lead his imaginary opponent to understanding by gradually reducing the acuity of his explanation. Only after the imaginary opponent fails to be persuaded by the reasoning of the intrinsic nature does Rongzom set forth the remaining three principles of reasoning. However, the traditional way to bring about insight in his opponent would involve exactly the opposite procedure: a gradual deepening of the profundity of reasoning where the argumentation is finally subsumed by the reasoning of the intrinsic nature. Such an approach would be in tune with the *Saṁdhinirmocanasūtra* and *Valid Means of Cognition*, and likewise with Jamgon Kongtrul's use of the principles.

A closer look at the structure of *Establishing Appearances as Divine* shows that the strongest and most significant statements are presented rather bluntly at the very beginning, while later in Rongzom's discourse the approach to persuasion is more gradual and conventional. The reason for Rongzom's change in the normative propaedeutic sequence might be his underlying Dzogchen perspective, although Mipham, equally a proponent of Dzogchen, does not highlight the principle of the intrinsic nature as the first in the set of arguments. Rongzom begins by stating his basic conviction through the reasoning of the intrinsic nature and only later does he retreat into a gradual treatment of the other three. In this way, he emphasizes the instantaneous approach to realization, where reasoning itself is transcended or "annulled" within the naked acknowledgment of the facts. In *Establishing Appearances as Divine,* the reasoning of the intrinsic nature is first applied to justify the well-known sūtric theorem that form is emptiness: If one were to wonder why form is empty, it is simply because that is its nature. Likewise, Rongzom subsequently states, all phenomena are naturally pure, the reason being that this simply is their nature.[191] Rongzom underscores the importance of the reasoning of the intrinsic nature (*chos nyid kyi rigs pa*), explaining it as the most fundamental and the final among the reasonings: "When something is proven with the reasoning of the intrinsic nature, one does not need to employ the three remaining [reasonings], for this one is the basis of the others, and it is the principal reasoning."[192]

Another possible explanation for the unusual sequence of reasoning might be that these principles, originally of a general mahāyānic nature, are here introduced in an esoteric context. In Mantrayāna, the result is taken as the path, meaning that the intrinsic nature is pointed out from the very beginning. Rongzom, wishing to express this, changes the Mahāyāna propaedeutic sequence of the four principles and rearranges them to form a propaedeutic method suitable for a comprehension of the Mantrayāna.

4.2 The Reasoning of Efficacy (*bya ba 'byed pa'i rigs pa, kāryakaranayukti*)

The remaining three reasonings are similarly treated in all the texts consulted for this study, and appear less enigmatic as principles of reason than the intrinsic nature. Instead of discussing them at length, we shall focus on Rongzom's definitions of the reasonings and their application in *Establishing Appearances as Divine* against the backdrop of definitions found in the classical sources cited earlier.

Rongzom's definition of the reasoning of efficacy in *Entering the Way of the Great Vehicle* is as follows:

> The reasoning of efficacy implies establishment with reference to the result.[193]

In *Establishing Appearances as Divine,* Rongzom is somewhat more specific:

> One comes to understand the causes of entities through their results. Just as one can observe that medicine and

> poison respectively perform the function of healing and killing, one comes to understand [the nature of] the agents by [considering] their function.[194]

The exclusion (*sel ba*) performed by this reasoning is explained as the elimination of "doubts regarding functions."[195] Rongzom also offers this critique:

> If the reasoning of efficacy is applied excessively, all actions and efforts will not be annulled, and in the end one will become a proponent of a creator being the cause.[196]

The definition found in the *Saṁdhinirmocanasūtra* reads:

> Certain causes and conditions function to bring about the acquisition, establishment, or arising of phenomena. This is the reasoning of efficacy .[197]

The *Abhidharmasamuccaya* defines the reasoning of efficacy in the following way:

> It is that phenomena that are by their own characteristics distinct each perform their own individual functions.[198]

Rongzom's definitions of the four reasonings are explained from the perspective of "the establisher," the subject (*sgrub byed yul can gyi rigs pa*). Although *Valid Means of Cognition* also defines this principle from the perspective of the establisher, its definition differs from Rongzom's: "The reasoning of efficacy is expressed with reference to functions and causes."[199] In this way, Rongzom's definitions differ considerably from the canonical definition in the *Saṁdhinirmocanasūtra,* as well as from Mipham's and Jamgon Kongtrul's definitions, which primarily define the reasonings with respect to the object (*gnas pa yul kyi rigs pa*). These latter sources generally confine themselves to pointing out the mere fact that particular causal factors assemble to produce particular effects. Rongzom, however, emphasizes that the result or function of a particular entity can tell us something about its cause or, by extension, the way that it truly is.

Rongzom employs the reasoning of efficacy as the second principle in *Establishing Appearances as Divine*, and this is also second in the canonical sequence. Every entity has a function and, according to Rongzom, an entity can therefore be appreciated with reference to its particular function and result. The purity of divinities or pure appearances can also be proven with reference to their particular function and result. We may infer that a certain substance possesses medicinal properties if we can observe that people who rely on it are cured of their disease. Likewise, we may infer that appearances are of a pure nature because we can observe that those who train in pure perception achieve pure accomplishments (*dngos grub, siddhi*) in the form of vajra body, speech, and mind. The observation of this "pure" function enables us to determine the pure nature of its cause.

Whether established with reference to causes or results, the principle of efficacy is observed when results are effectuated due to the completion of their nexus of causes and conditions. The reasoning of efficacy is, in this way, closely tied to the reasoning of dependency.

4.3 The Reasoning of Dependency (*ltos pa'i rigs pa, apekṣāyukti*)

A result depends on the full assemblage of its causes and conditions, and conventions (*tha snyad, vyahāra*) similarly appear interdependently, as with "long" and "short." In *Entering the Way of the*

Great Vehicle, Rongzom succinctly defines this principle of reasoning with reference to its subjective aspect: "The reasoning of dependency is to establish with reference to a cause."[200] *Valid Means of Cognition,* on the other hand, explains that this principle refers to "the expression of reasoning with regard to phenomena and results."[201] The *Saṁdhinirmocanasūtra* characteristically defines this reasoning in an objective sense: "The reasoning of dependency consists of the causes and conditions for conditioned phenomena and the subsequent construction of conventions."[202] Similarly, the *Abhidharmasamuccaya* refers to the objective aspect in stating, "when conditioned [phenomena] arise they do so depending on circumstances."[203]

Rongzom explains the exclusion (*sel ba*) performed by the principle of dependency as the dispelling of "doubts regarding the thorough formation [of things]."[204] He warns about possible excesses: "If the reasoning of dependency is applied excessively, all [factors of] capability will not be annulled, and in the end one will become a proponent of the Almighty being the cause."[205] Cautious about accepting conventionalities such as results depending on causes, Rongzom again underscores the temporary and pragmatic value of reasoning.

Having defined this principle as a reasoning that effectuates recognition of results with reference to their causes, Rongzom continues in *Establishing Appearances as Divine*: "It establishes origination, as with the establishment of the sprout based on a seed. Alternatively, it establishes conventions, as with the establishment of the convention of good based on evil."[206] Rongzom points out that all phenomena are mental appearances (*sems kyi snang ba*) and therefore all purity and impurity are resultant appearances that depend on the mind as their cause. Both pure and impure experiences are equally real in being results produced by the mind. However, the reasoning of dependency leads Rongzom to conclude that pure appearances must be more valid than impure ones.[207]

4.4 The Reasoning of Valid Proof (*'thad pa sgrub pa'i rigs pa, upapattisādhanayukti*)

The principle of valid proof features last in Rongzom's list, while the *Saṁdhinirmocanasūtra* and the other texts consulted here present it as number three. In *Entering the Way of the Great Vehicle,* this reasoning is defined in the following way:

> The reasoning of valid proof is that which establishes by way of making reasoning itself free from stain.[208]

The *Abhidharmasamuccaya* terms this principle the "reasoning of proving argument" (*gtan tshigs sgrub pa'i rigs pa*) rather than "reasoning of valid proof" (*'thad pa sgrub pa'i rigs pa*), defining it as "the demonstration of the established meaning as not being in conflict with *pramāṇa*."[209] *Valid Means of Cognition* similarly uses the term "reasoning of logical proof" (*gtan tshigs sgrub pa'i rigs pa*):

> The reasoning establishing logical arguments is omniapplicable [throughout argumentation] as it demonstrates the various defining characteristics of proof.[210]

Finally, the *Saṁdhinirmocanasūtra* explains the principle in the following way:

> The reasoning of valid proof establishes meanings known, taught, or asserted. It consists of the causes and conditions for thorough understanding.[211]

Rongzom explains the exclusion performed by this principle as "the dispelling of doubts regarding reasoning itself,"[212] and again he warns against taking this reasoning too far: "If the reasoning of valid proof is applied excessively, then [one's] reasoning will become stain[less] in any situation, and in the end, one will become haughtily arrogant."[213]

In *Establishing Appearances as Divine,* Rongzom specifies that if a probandum has already been established through the first three types of reasoning, there is no need for the principle of valid proof. However, if that is not the case, this principle can prove the validity of an argument by reference to the subject (*chos can, dharmin*), a probandum (*sgrub bya, sādhya*), an example (*dpe, dṛṣṭānta*), and a reversed pervasion (*ldog khyab, vyatirekavyāpti*). Thus, this principle is associated with the traditional three modes (*tshul gsum, trairūpya*) of autonomous inference (*rang rgyud kyi rjes dpag, svātantrānumāna*). Rongzom elaborately employs this principle in his proof of divine appearances by means of what he calls "instantaneous and gradual establishment" (*cig car dang rim gyis sgrup pa*). He cites a scriptural authority (*lung, āgama*) and attempts to demonstrate its validity by rearranging it to display the "three modes" (*tshul gsum, trairūpya*) in autonomous inference.[214] Rongzom explains the instantaneous and gradual ways of establishing purity using the example of humans and hungry ghosts, who perceive their own dramatically different versions of the same object: humans see water, while spirits see pus. It can, however, be proven to hungry ghosts that what they see is, in fact, not pus but water. For individuals with little attachment (*zhen pa chung ba*), there is no need to first establish a temporary validity of the subject under investigation as it is commonly perceived by hungry ghosts, and in this case the establishment is instantaneous. If, however, a commonly shared basis for experience must first be established as perceived by hungry ghosts, the establishment is of a gradual character. In both cases, Rongzom applies autonomous inference as his logical technique.

To sum up, Rongzom's treatment of the four principles appears unconventional, innovative, and yet also cautious. He predominantly considers the subjective aspects of these logical principles and in each case warns about their potential shortcomings. He changes the canonical sequence of the four principles and begins his exegesis with the reasoning of the intrinsic nature (*chos nyid kyi rigs pa*), both in *Establishing Appearances as Divine* and in *Entering the Way of the Great Vehicle.* We have treated the principle of the intrinsic nature quite elaborately here in view of its philosophical intricacy and Rongzom's unconventional presentation of the topic. Although Rongzom devotes considerable space to explaining the four principles and uses them in *Establishing Appearances as Divine* to grant validity to the esoteric theorem of purity, he also questions both the scope and usefulness of reasoning as such.

To conclude our discussion of the four principles of reasoning, we now turn to Mipham's treatment of purity, allegedly inspired by Rongzom.

4.5 Rongzom's Influence on Mipham's Epistemological Account of Purity

Rongzom employs the four principles of reasoning to establish the validity of pure appearances. In this way, he seeks to prove that purity and divinity abide as the natural condition of things (*dngos po'i gnas lugs*). As we investigate the influence of Rongzom's proofs of purity on his followers, we shall focus primarily on Mipham and his commentators. With his twofold division of the conventional valid cognition (*kun tu tha snyad pa'i tshad ma*), impure confined seeing (*ma dag tshur mthong tshad ma*)[215] versus pure vision (*rnam *dag dag gzigs tshad ma*), Mipham brings the issue of purity to the forefront of his epistemology. In the *Survey of the Guhyagarbha Tantra*, Mipham explains:

> Therefore, to briefly demonstrate this extremely profound key point, there are two conventional valid cognitions. There are two, because there is conventional valid cognition based on confined seeing just as there is conventional valid cognition based on pure vision. If one were to briefly explain the difference between them then this can be understood by considering their cause, essence, function, and result. The first [the valid cognition of confined vision] arises based on a correct examination of its particular object, which is of a limited nature. That is how it is caused. In essence it is, on the occasion, an undeceiving awareness of merely its own object. Its function is the exclusion of superimpositions with regard to its object [as cognized by] confined seeing. The result is engagement based on having determined the object of the particular context.
>
> As for the latter, [the valid cognition of pure seeing] is attained after having correctly observed the intrinsic nature just as it is. This is its cause. Its essence is vast *prajñā* with respect to all possible subjects [to be cognized]. Its function is to exclude superimpositions with regard to the field of experience that is inconceivable to the confined perception of an ordinary mind stream. The result is the accomplishment of omniscient wisdom.[216]

According to Mipham, pure appearances possess a veridical value that, being perceived by a superior *pramāṇa*, supersedes that of impure phenomena.[217] The valid cognition of pure appearances belongs to the category of the conventional (*tha snyad*) and can, hence, provide validity to the relative truth of great purity as asserted in Mahāyoga.

Mipham's commentator Do-ngag Tenpay Nyima elaborates on the consequences of lacking such a *pramāṇa* and states that valid cognitions, as set forth in the *Pramāṇavārttika,* can merely ascertain impure phenomena and not the properties of purity.[218] He goes on to state the necessity of positing the valid cognition of pure seeing and the flaws incurred by not acknowledging it. He remarks that the *sugatagarbha*, the great purity of Mahāyoga, and the spontaneous presence of Atiyoga all come down to a mere hypothesis without this valid cognition of pure seeing.[219] Do-ngag Tenpay Nyima then argues that while reasonings, such as the five classical Madhyamaka arguments, can prove the ultimately empty aspect of appearances, there is no way to prove the relative great purity, the aspect of luminosity, apart from the valid cognition of pure vision. This clarifies the strong emphasis that post-Mipham Nyingma proponents place on the ability to establish esoteric theorems by means of a particular *pramāṇa*—an emphasis on reasoning in the esoteric context that they tend to trace back to Rongzom and his *Establishing Appearances as Divine.*

Mipham and his Nyingma interpreters all contend that the *pramāṇa* of pure vision is not Mipham's innovation, but a characteristic approach of the school's forefathers. For instance, Karma Phuntsho has proposed that the way of ascertaining the nature of all phenomena—by considering the way they appear and the way they are, as well as their relative and ultimate aspects—through four valid cognitions[220] is an extraordinary feature of the Early Translations.[221] On several occasions, Mipham's commentator Do-ngag Tenpay Nyima similarly contends that the division into four types of valid cognition is a key feature of the approach of the early masters that is absent in the New Schools.[222]

The set of four valid cognitions appears to be absent from the work of any Nyingma philosopher prior to Mipham, and so it is noteworthy that the Nyingma school attributes the origin of the fourfold distinction to the Early Dissemination period (*snga dar*), a thousand years prior to Mipham's compositions. It seems reasonable that this attribution was a move to provide authority to novel principles by ascribing them to earlier masters, a move that many Indo-Tibetan Buddhist philosophers have felt authorized to make[223] when they believed that their innovations were implied by, and so contained within, the teachings of the forefathers of the tradition. The early fountainheads of the tradition may in this way have inspired Mipham to split conventional *pramāṇa* into two, so as to "clarify Rongzom's intent." Rongzom's continuous criticism of the Madhyamaka's authentic relative truth as an obstruction to the realization of purity[224] may have inspired Mipham to posit a second conventional *pramāṇa* to negate the impure properties of the authentic relative and account for the validity of divine appearances. Troshul Jamdor formulates it this way: "This establishment of apparent objects as naturally being maṇḍalas of deities is little known in the New Translation schools, and is the unique tradition of the Early Translation School. This emphasis is the eloquent lion's roar of the great paṇḍita, the omniscient Rongzom."[225] In the *Beacon of Certainty* Mipham himself explains:

> The natural state is the exclusive truth of unity
> And valid cognition is self-existing wakefulness,
> Besides being unaware there is nothing to be abandoned,
> And [thus, all comes down to] simply awareness and lack of awareness.

> Therefore, with this tradition of valid cognition,
> All appearances are established naturally as divinities.
> This is exclusively our tradition, The Early Translations,
> The lion's roar, the excellent explanations
> Of the omniscient Rongzom Paṇḍita.[226]

Here, we see Mipham proclaiming his reliance on Rongzom in positing the *pramāṇa* that evaluates purity. Considering Rongzom's emphasis on the validity of purity, a link of inspiration between Rongzom and Mipham seems likely.

In the *Beacon of Certainty,* Mipham refers to this as he once more acknowledges Rongzom as an extraordinary authority:

> The analysis of other vehicles' philosophical systems
> Reveals their progressive purity, which culminates here [in the Great Perfection].
> Thus the way this is established
> Through the valid cognition of stainless wisdom
> Is found in all the interpretative commentaries and tantras
> And in the analysis of Dharmabhadra.[227]

Mipham not only refers to Rongzom (Dharmabhadra, i.e., Rongzom Chökyi Zangpo), but also to the tantras and their commentaries in general. It is telling, however, that among all tantric literature, Mipham exclusively specifies Rongzom's analytical approach.

We may by now wonder whether there is a fundamental difference between the Nyingma view of purity (as evinced in the writings of philosophers such as Rongzom and Mipham) and the approach of New Schools such as the Gelug, with whom Mipham often debated. Mipham argues clearly against the position that one should imagine purity while still retaining a concept of the actual reality being impure.[228] In the *Survey of the Guhyagarbha Tantra* he says:

> In this way, through the path of the two stages the stains are cleared and consequently the natural state is actualized. Yet, if this purity would not be natural, one would, through the development stage, be mentally creating something that is in conflict with the abiding way and, [during the completion stage,] one would be stopping the prāṇa within one's ordinary body. When, through such types of [exercises], all entities for accomplishment manifest as divinities in one's own perception, then these would be nothing but deluded appearances. They would have nothing in common with the [actual] entities and be comparable to [the appearance of] magical horses and elephants where there are [in fact only] pebbles. Such an apprehension would be an erroneous cognition (*log shes*). Since also taking the five poisons onto the path and the conduct free of acceptance and rejection would be in a similar [discord with reality], the assertion that such a path is superior to the sūtric path would be extremely astonishing!
>
> If the difference between Sūtra and Mantra lies only in what is simply skillful means and not in the view, then why were such easy and effective means not taught also in the sūtras! Therefore, since in the causal vehicles the view of spontaneous presence of cause and effect is absent, one must understand that [followers of the causal vehicle] are temporarily not [proper] vessels to whom such means can be imparted. All those who do not know the ontological fact of the primordial great pure equality,

> and propose that through mere methods sentient beings can be forcefully transformed into Buddhas, will not be able to accomplish the path of the two stages where one trains in accordance with the abiding way of entities. One must understand that such individuals severely denigrate the Mantrayāna.[229]

Mipham is adamant in advocating the intrinsic purity of all phenomena and rebukes the idea of purity or divinities being merely skillful means (*thabs*), an approach already evident in Rongzom's *Establishing Appearances as Divine*. Nyingma scholars such as Rongzom and Mipham distinguish themselves from the New Schools by attempting to provide dialectical foundations for the tantric concept of purity. Mipham treats purity as an issue of fundamental concern, just as Rongzom did, and allocates a specific valid cognition that ascertains the genuine veridical value of purity. Rongzom, on the other hand, establishes purity through the four principles of reasoning. Although their methodological approaches differ, the outcome of their pursuits is identical. Purity is not just an expedient means but, in itself, an aspect of reality that must be acknowledged accordingly.

· 5 ·

Conclusion

THE ELEVENTH CENTURY witnessed the flourishing of many new practice lineages from India, as well as the emergence of a skeptical attitude towards the esoteric teachings imported during the early dissemination. Rongzom, an advocate of the Early Translations, was active during this century and would have witnessed the mounting criticism of these teachings. One of the emerging trends of the eleventh century was a marked emphasis on the study of epistemology and logic, found in places such as the monastery of Sangphu. Rongzom, either inspired or provoked by this trend, applies logico-epistemological tools in his discourse, thereby bringing the esoteric Nyingma teachings into a normative discourse with the exoteric teachings. Whether Rongzom wished to defend the Nyingma teachings in the face of criticism or simply felt attracted to logical discourse is difficult to ascertain. In any case, Rongzom comes across as a self-confident writer who produced a large literary output despite facing criticism.

Although for Rongzom the view of Mantra is clearly superior to that of Sūtra, he does not discard the logical principles of the exoteric teachings but instead introduces them into the esoteric contexts of his exegetical discourse. In positing a superior veridical value for

Mantra, Rongzom juxtaposes the Mantra view with a Madhyamaka philosophy that may, despite the almost certain anachronism, be described as Svātantrika. Rongzom primarily critiques the Madhyamaka school for its objectification of the relative truth and the subsequent separation of the two truths. We have here interpreted this critique as a sign of Rongzom's firm commitment to purity as an expression of reality and have found in his Madhyamaka critique a hermeneutical link to his Mahāyoga exposition of purity and equality (*dag mnyam*). For Rongzom, the Madhyamaka objectification (however temporary or relative) of the impure characteristics of the authentic relative, and the related need to negate these characteristics in order to realize the ultimate (*don dam*, *paramārtha*), hinders the realization of a relative purity that is inseparable from ultimate equality. Thus, the two truths in their Madhyamaka interpretation lose their equal veridical value, becoming isolated from one another in a way that goes against both the nature of things and the teachings of Mantra.

Although Rongzom does not discuss any Madhyamaka school that can be identified as, or compared to, what later became known as Prāsaṅgika, Mipham, who sees himself as a follower of Rongzom, nevertheless claims to have based his own explanation of the Svātantrika/Prāsaṅgika distinction on Rongzom's exegesis. Through contrasting Rongzom's tantra-based criticism with Mipham's Prāsaṅgika interpretation, it has been argued that Mipham does take into account Rongzom's explanations on Madhyamaka, albeit without reference to an explicit treatment of Svātantrika/Prāsaṅgika, as such a discussion is altogether absent from Rongzom's extant works. Instead Mipham relates to Rongzom's tantra-based Madhyamaka critique. In positing an inseparability of two equally *svabhāva*-less truths, this Madhyamaka critique is indeed resonant with Mipham's Candrakīrti interpretation. Considering Rongzom's straightforward and direct objections to Madhyamaka and his advocacy of the superiority of the view of Mantra, he saw no reason to justify his tantric views by appealing to a more readily acceptable Madhyamaka perspective. Unlike Mipham, Rongzom did not attempt to harmonize the view of Mantra or Dzogchen with Madhyamaka.

While not defending Dzogchen and Mantra by harmonizing these teachings with Madhyamaka, Rongzom nevertheless, in *Establishing Appearances as Divine*, promotes the purity of all appearances through the four principles of reasoning. His treatment of these four principles is unconventional, pragmatic, and also cautious. Rongzom does not hesitate to integrate dialectics into his assessment of Dzogchen and Mantra and yet concomitantly demonstrates a deep ambiguity toward the capacity and relevance of reasoning itself. In the context of the four principles, we have also considered how Mipham again is influenced by Rongzom's proofs of purity as he allocates a specific *pramāṇa* for the verification of purity and divinity.

Prominent Nyingma masters throughout the ages have held that the view of Mantra is superior to that of Sūtra. To them, Sūtra lacks the acknowledgment of factors such as purity, divine luminosity, and the inseparability of the two truths. Insofar as purity and divinities are not merely skillful means but central to the view of reality, their assessment by reasoning is more pertinent for the Nyingma proponent than for a follower of the New Schools, who would consider Madhyamaka alone the perfect view. The main thrust of Rongzom's dialectical reasoning is not aimed at establishing the view of Madhyamaka, which he criticizes. Instead he focuses on esoteric theorems that he seeks to verify through the tools of the exoteric vehicle. This is how, as a follower of the *Guhyagarbha Tantra* and Dzogchen during a time of skepticism towards the tantras of the imperial period, Rongzom proceeds to "establish appearances as divine." In doing this, he laid out the path for future Nyingma scholars who, like himself, would set the view of Mantra apart from Sūtra by acknowledging purity, divinity, and luminosity, and who also regarded purity not just as a means to a result, but as the nature of the result itself.

More sustained and systematic research is clearly called for to investigate further the degree to which Rongzom inspired later Nyingma scholars in their view of purity, their distinction between Sūtra and Mantra, and the role they ascribe to reasoning in the esoteric context. Likewise, there is a strong need for further studies of the Indic and early Tibetan tantric movements that were received by Rongzom himself. When did reasoning begin to find a distinct application on the esoteric level, and how might this tendency be connected with a superior view of Mantra? At this point I simply wish that these reflections on Rongzom and his views on purity, Madhyamaka, and reasoning may lead to more in-depth studies of Rongzom's rich and extraordinary works.

Translation and Comparative Edition of

Establishing Appearances as Divine

◆ ◆ ◆

Establishing Appearances as Divine According to the Secret Mantra, the Vajra Vehicle

THE VAJRA VEHICLE of Secret Mantra states, "all mundane and supramundane phenomena, without any distinction, are primordially enlightened as the maṇḍala of vajralike body, speech, and mind. Thus [the maṇḍala] is not accomplished through a path."[230]

Here one may object, "all those phenomena that appear within the field of experience of sentient beings are not as they seem to be. They are delusion, and thus they cannot be primordial enlightenment."[231] Yes, this is nothing but delusion. Besides this delusion of sentient beings, there is nothing else which might be posited and shown. These phenomena, known as delusion, are all that there is.[232]

Now, non-Buddhists (*tīrthikas*) impute the existence of a permanent personal self, while some Vaibhāṣikas believe that the person exists within the characteristics of impermanence. Other Vaibhāṣikas and the Sautrāntikas negate the personal self, while claiming the existence of the characteristics of phenomena, such as the aggregates, which are empty of [that] self. The Yogācārins believe that the dependent nature is empty of any imputation and that, along with its emptiness, the dependent nature exists. The Mādhyamikas assert that all phenomena are ultimately free from the extremes of existence, nonexistence, and so forth, and in this way they cut completely through mental constructs. According to the Secret Mantra, the two truths are inseparable and primordial enlightenment.[233] Thus, wandering beings set forth their individual views and argue about them based on the characteristics of their shared perception, and there are, hence, not separate subjects [for investigation].[234]

In this way, all apparent phenomena are nothing but delusion and there is, moreover, no freedom from delusion to be achieved by dispelling delusion. Delusion is, by its own essence, completely pure and, hence, enlightened.[235] All phenomena are, in this way, primordially, fully, and completely enlightened. Phenomena appearing as various attributes are, therefore, indeed the maṇḍala of vajra body, speech, and mind. They are like the Buddhas of the three times, never transcending the essence of complete purity. Sentient beings and Buddhas are not differentiated in terms of their essence. Just like distinct causes and results appearing in a dream, they are nothing but perceptions of individual minds brought forth by the power of imputation.

Here the issue might be raised, "although the scriptures do teach this, there is no certainty whether it is to be taken at face value[236] or requires interpretation. Therefore the essential purity of phenomena may well be established, but it is unreasonable to say that precisely the nature of that which appears as subjects with attributes is primordially enlightened.[237] For, if it were that way, thorough affliction and saṃsāra would be entirely absent. There can't be a reasoning that establishes such a philosophy." The conceptual mind that takes objects that appear in the experience of sentient beings as valid is, since beginningless time, deluded. It accepts or negates with reference to the way things appear to it. With such dialectics it is, indeed, not possible to establish the vast and profound meaning. Nevertheless, since the nature of phenomena is inconceivable, it is not the case that there is no way to realize it by means of discriminating knowledge. Thus it is not in any way a mistake if one, rather than that, is inclined to approach simply by faith, regarding the scriptures and oral instructions as valid. One will then gain access through trust.[238]

One may object, "Well, if one cannot prove [the primordial maṇḍala] with reasoning, one cannot gain access to it either."[239] We can prove it as follows: That phenomena are fully enlightened as the maṇḍala of vajra body, speech, and mind is proven with the reasoning of the intrinsic nature.[240] Just as it is stated in a sūtra, "Form is empty by nature. Why is that? It is so because that is its nature." All phenomena are pure by their intrinsic nature and, therefore, there is not a single phenomenon that is impure. This is the intrinsic nature of phenomena. Complete purity is, therefore, also the intrinsic nature of body, speech, and mind, and their complete purity is enlightenment. Therefore, body, speech, and mind, distinguished by their complete purity, are inseparable, free from mental constructs, and perfectly pervasive. One must in this way understand them to be the maṇḍala of vajra body, speech, and mind. When something is proven with the reasoning of the intrinsic nature, one does not need to employ the three remaining [reasonings], for this one is the basis of the others, and it is the principal reasoning.[241]

Again it may be asked, "Since, for us, this intrinsic nature is not established, you will need to prove it by means of other reasonings." Well then, so be it. Regarding the reasoning of efficacy,[242] one comes to understand the causes of all entities by means of their results. Just as one can observe that medicine and poison respectively perform the function of healing or killing, one comes to understand [the nature of] the agents by [considering] their function. Likewise, it is observed that one who meditates on the maṇḍala of vajra body, speech, and mind will attain the siddhi of pure body, speech, and mind. Apparent phenomena are, thus, with reference to their function, powerfully established as being in essence vajra body, speech, and mind. This establishment is not [claimed] by mere argument without relying on the power of fact. Consider this example: A person who finds a wish-fulfilling jewel, but has in the past never used it for his enjoyment, may not recognize it to be a wish-fulfilling jewel. He may believe it to be an ordinary jewel, not seeing its good qualities. Later, a person learned in the different types of jewels may point out [the nature of that jewel], clean the jewel, and make it an object of veneration. Only then will its extraordinary qualities become evident. Through observing its extraordinary [wish-fulfilling] function, it will be understood with certainty that it is a precious jewel. Likewise, unless ordinary body, speech, and mind are understood to be divine, and revered [as divine], their [divine] qualities will not be seen. However, it is observed that [divine] qualities manifest wherever [body, speech, and mind] are understood and revered [as divine].

[The pure nature of things] can equally be established through the reasoning of dependency.[243] The reasoning of dependency makes one understand a resultant entity based on its causes. It establishes origination, as when proving that based on a seed there is a sprout. It also establishes conventions, as when establishing the convention of good based on evil. Likewise, all phenomena appear as the features of the mind itself and, therefore, it is established that both pure and impure results arise in dependence on their cause, the mind. Both the pure and the impure field of experience are, thus, products of the mind's habitual patterns, and, hence, both of those are established as genuine. As for which one of the two is deluded and which not deluded, this is proven by the reasoning of dependency. One must, therefore, certainly understand that the appearances of the pure field of experience are established to be the genuine ones.

If proven in this way by the three reasonings, there is no need to prove anything through the reasoning of valid proof, for beyond those reasonings of intrinsic nature, cause, and result there are no logical arguments of direct perception or inference.[244]

One might wonder, "Of what use, then, is this reasoning of valid proof?" For those of inferior capacity, reasoning itself is to be established first, for that is the means by which they must evaluate the meaning, and proof must, thus, be made by means of a definite subject, probandum, example, and forward and reverse pervasion.[245]

Again it might be argued, "For some people, this alone may be enough proof. But, since there are some who will not be convinced unless things are proven through the reasoning of valid proof, you must make use of that!"[246] Let me first prove by means of scripture that it is established [as valid] for both [parties in the debate].[247] In the *Viṣayāvatārajñānālokālaṁkārasūtra*[248] it is said:

> Phenomena, always unborn, are the Thus-gone-one.
> All phenomena are like the Bliss-gone-one.
> Those with childish intellect grasp at attributes,
> And thus, within the worlds, relate to phenomena that do not exist.

The statement that phenomena, always unborn, are the Thus-gone-one is the logical argument.[249] "All phenomena" is the subject and "are like the Bliss-gone-one" is the example. The probandum is the establishment of all phenomena to be the Thus-gone-one.

One might wonder whether this may not be impaired by direct perception. In response it is stated, "Those with childish intellect grasp at attributes, and thus, within the world, relate to phenomena that do not exist."[250] Infantile and verbally untrained individuals may take the visual distortion of falling hairs [to be actual hairs] and they may happily partake of [the experience of] a wheel that appears [when] a firebrand [is moved quickly in a circle]. Likewise, childish, ordinary beings experience by apprehending attributes of objects that are imputed by their deluded consciousnesses. Their experience thus comes down to nothing but an experience of objects that are not there. The proof is, therefore, as follows: All phenomena are the Thus-gone-one, because phenomena, always unborn, are the Thus-gone-one, just like the Bliss-gone-ones of the three times.[251] In what way are [all phenomena] like [the Bliss-gone-ones]? The Bliss-gone-one is not differentiated with respect to body, speech, and mind. He is differentiated with respect to the intrinsic nature. Just as it is said that, "The noble being is the one differentiated by the unconditioned," it is thus through obtaining the unconditioned that all the noble ones achieve their very nobleness. In the same way, phenomena are the Thus-gone-one, because of obtaining the nature of the unconditioned. The objects of the experience of marks are unlike this. While there is nothing, those who wish to experience are simply engaging in phenomena that do not exist.

It may be asked, "Well then, phenomena may by their essential nature be established as the identity of enlightenment, but what reasoning of valid proof is available to establish the maṇḍala of vajra body, speech, and mind from the perspective of mere appearance?"[252] Thus we must prove. The proof can either be given instantaneously or gradually.[253] Those with little attachment to their own experience will arrive at an understanding through instantaneous proof, and for them I shall first of all give an example. Hungry ghosts perceive rivers to be filled with pus. Some among them will also have heard that human beings perceive water. Among them, some may, thus, believe that pus is the genuine entity and that water is an imputed form.[254] Others may believe that pus is an impure appearance and that, therefore, water, as perceived by humans, is what genuinely [exists]. The [latter group] will argue, saying, "Friends, this river, filled with pus, as perceived in common by us hungry ghosts, is, in fact, a river of water as perceived by humans. For, if somebody who has free access to that water dedicates the water to us and gives it to us, we hungry ghosts will also perceive, and experience, it as water. It is just like that water we have obtained from time to time in the past." With respect to the establishment of relation,[255] such establishment is, in this case, flawless: "That which is dedicated and given by the one who has free access to water, and that which, thus, comes to be experienced as water, is indeed water, just like the water that we have heard of from time to time." Thus the statement "If those with free access to water dedicate it and then give it to us, we experience it as water" is established with certain pervasion.

In the same way, some individuals will have heard that the appearances of bodies and enjoyments, as commonly perceived by humans, can be perceived by people of complete purity as a divine maṇḍala. Moreover, they also know that, according to Secret Mantra, [everything] is taught to be the divine maṇḍala. Some will argue that the appearances of ordinary bodies and enjoyments are genuine entities, while the seeing of divinities is an imputation and so on. Others will believe ordinary bodies and enjoyments to be impure appearances and that divinity as seen by pure individuals and as renowned in the Secret Mantra is therefore the genuine characteristic of entities.

The [latter group] will say, "Dear friends, these appearances of ordinary bodies and enjoyments commonly perceived by us human beings are, in fact, the divine maṇḍala as perceived by pure individuals. If an individual who has free access to the field of pure experience grants us accomplishment, then, even to us human beings, those objects will appear as divinities and we will experience them as such. It is just like when, from time to time in the past, some of us human beings gained accomplishment and thereby achieved the divine field of experience." If one were to demonstrate the relation, then it would prove to be a faultless one. Again, when someone who has gained free access to the field of pure experience grants accomplishment, that which is then enjoyed as the divine field of experience is indeed divine, just like the divine field of experience achieved by an accomplished individual. As for this ordinary field of experience, if individuals who have free access to the completely pure field of experience grant accomplishment, then there will be an experience of divine objects. The proof is thus established with certain pervasion.

This cannot be invalidated by direct perception either, for [the deluded mind] is obscured by karmic veils.[256] For example, once in the past the gods were moved to feel compassion for a destitute girl of this world, yet when they granted her gold it would only appear as coal [to her]. [However, the gold] would gradually appear to those who possessed the link of compassion and karma. Thus, when a bit of the gold that was given by the Fire God appeared to the poor girl, she was able to use it for her enjoyment.[257]

In the same way, if the perception of those who are extremely attached to their own perception is not first established as true, they will not [be able to] engage with the very basis [for investigation].[258] Therefore, first one establishes their own perception as true and then lets them gradually gain access to extraordinary philosophies. As for the way to do this, we may take the previous example of the two hungry ghosts with differing views. One argues, "This river filled with pus, commonly perceived by us, possesses not only the characteristics of pus, but also those of water, because what appears are the features of the mind. It is just as in the case of the water which was obtained [earlier] through dedication and the [presently] perceived pus." Also, "Whatever is a feature of the mind is in all respects characterized by being appearance, just like the water obtained through dedication and the ordinary appearance of pus. This great river of pus is also the appearance of the mind's features. There are thus no different features, since they accord in being the common appearance of fluidity[259] just as it is the case with the perceived pus." If established in this way, this reasoning will make sense to an individual who believes that appearances are mind.

Once one has in this way established [the two appearances] as being equal, one goes on to refute the characteristics of pus. It is indeed true that these two are equal in being apparent features of the mind, but, since the appearance of pus is impure, it is delusion. Water is a pure appearance and, therefore, not delusion. In this way whatever is delusion is impure and that which is impure is delusion.[260] This [demonstrates] equal pervasion. Purity and nondelusion should be viewed in the same way. Through this very argument in which there is certain pervasion, [we can establish that] the pus is a delusive appearance or an appearance of delusion, while the water is not delusive, an appearance that is free from delusion. Likewise, from the point of view of all phenomena being merely illusory appearances, all that appears to ordinary wandering beings—bodies and enjoyments as subsumed within body, speech, and mind—is not exclusively the nature of suffering. Neither is it exclusively the characteristics of the basis for the arising of afflictions. It is also the characteristics of enlightenment, just as they appear to pure individuals—the realm and field of experience that is of completely pure identity and subsumed within the vajra body, speech, and mind—because this is the appearance of the features of the mind, just like the divinities perceived by somebody who has gained sacred accomplishment and the vases, pillars, etc. that are perceived by an ordinary individual.

Whatever is a feature of the mind is in all respects characterized by being appearance, just like the divinities that appear to some, and pillars and so on that appear to others. The bodies, abodes, and enjoyments that appear to ordinary individuals as objects are also the appearance of the mind's features. There are not different features, because these [appearances] accord in being the appearances of bodies, abodes, and enjoyment, subsumed as [ordinary] body, speech, and mind, just like the appearance of pillars, etc. If established in this way, this reasoning will be proven to an individual who believes that appearances are mind.

Once [the two appearances] have been established in this way as being equal, one goes on to refute the characteristics of suffering. It is indeed true that these two are equal in being apparent features of the mind, but since the appearances of suffering and the bases of suffering are impure, they are delusion. Liberation and the bases of liberation are pure appearances and, therefore, not delusion. Whatever is delusion is impure and whatever is impure is delusion. This [demonstrates] equal pervasion. Purity and nondelusion should be viewed in the same way. Through precisely this logical argument in which there is certain pervasion, the appearances to ordinary [perception] are shown to be a delusion, or deluded perceptions, while the appearances of divinities are not delusion, or are appearances free from delusion. This should be realized with certainty.

I shall now elaborate a bit on the statement that the features [of purity and impurity] are not different [from each other]. Some believe, "If one meditates on vases, pillars, etc. as divinities, it is indeed so that they will appear as divinities endowed with enlightened body, speech, and mind, but those are then not the [actual] characteristics of the pillars, etc. It is the same as when one meditates on repulsiveness and the entire ground [appears to be] filled with bones and so forth.[261] In the same way as the appearance resulting from the meditation on the perception spheres of totality is a mastered form, a particular within the sense source of mental phenomena, it therefore [does] not [constitute] the characteristics of an [actual] entity."[262] Others will object, saying that when divinities appear, then that which appears cannot be the characteristics of shared appearances, because this is but one's own perception that has been transformed.

The reply to those objections is that the features [of purity and impurity] are not different, because they are commonly shared appearance. Just as that which appears as pus to hungry ghosts is the personal experience of those with similar karma, so is the appearance of water the personal experience of those with similar karma. Therefore, it is not permissible to refer to these as different bases.[263] It is not wrong that they both accord in appearing as fluidity. Hence, it is feasible to posit the river as the subject. If one were to object to this too,[264] then since the very appearance of pus is, [in fact], the private experience of an individual, one would fail to find anything that is established for both proponent and opponent. Similarly the impure appearances of body, speech, and mind apparent to ordinary perception and the pure appearances of the realm and field of experience of the divine vajra body, speech, and mind are both irreversibly commonly shared perceptions. Therefore, it is in this way feasible to posit appearances as the subject [for debate]. If, on the other hand, one negates shared appearances, asserting that since the appearances are [nothing but] individual perceptions they are all different, then since the pillar, etc. are [also nothing but] individual perceptions, it will be impossible to find anything at all that is established for both parties in the debate. Therefore, when establishing appearances to be divine, the fault of having different subjects is not present.[265]

The following question might be raised: "Is not the deity of complete purity distinguished and posited with reference to the intrinsic nature and wisdom? How could it be the appearance of the features of the mind?" The deity of complete purity can be set forth in two ways. A reflection in a mirror may, by virtue of being a quality of the mirror, be said to pertain to the mirror, and by virtue of being the reflection of one's face, it may be said to pertain to the face. Likewise, the appearances of divine body, speech, and mind are perceived by the power of realizing the intrinsic nature by wisdom and by the force of compassion and aspiration prayers. Therefore they are distinguished by wisdom and the intrinsic nature.[266] The divine appearances are, however, also the appearances of the features of the mind and its habitual tendencies, and therefore they also come down to [simply] mind.[267]

One might wonder how habitual tendencies[268] cause these to appear. [First of all] there is the habitual tendency of the two types of apprehending, which manifest as object and subject. Through the habitual tendency of white karma, extraordinary ornaments, such as the major and minor marks, become apparent. Furthermore, the habitual tendency of believing in a self causes oneself and the divine continuum to appear different from each other and creates a raw split between [oneself and] the objects. The habitual tendency of full expression creates the appearance of different attributes. The habitual tendency of the links of existence creates the appearance of the nature of birth, yet the exhaustion of all habitual tendencies without exception will not bring about the appearance of the utterly pure field of experience.[269] One may, likewise, examine whether the mundane wisdom of pure enlightenment [270] is existent or nonexistent, but [in fact] it is an inconceivable quality.

Again an objection might be raised, "It is posited that the completely pure deity is the identity of the object. Yet that which is distinguished by wisdom and the intrinsic nature cannot be present within the identity of that which is the appearance of the ordinary mind's delusion." This is also not true. Even the mind of an ordinary being is naturally characterized by complete purification. And wisdom is not exclusively dependent on the development of bodhicitta either. Sūtras that are established [as valid] for both of us explain the establishment of self-existing wisdom. The noble *Prajñāpāramitāsūtra* states:

> Even the mind of an ordinary being
> Is by nature complete purification.

In the chapter on the turning of the wheel in the abode of the divine youth Suyāma, the *Gandharvyūhasūtra* teaches:

> Numerous worlds may burn up
> In the most inconceivable way,
> Yet space cannot be burned.
> So it is, also, with self-existing wisdom.

One could bring more citations renowned in the tradition of Secret Mantra, but this suffices. Therefore, since the completely coarse [i.e., not subtle] obscurations have been completely purified, completely pure fields and objects will be perceived, although most of the commonly shared appearances will not have disappeared.[271] Therefore, the subject [that which appears as either pure or impure] is not different [in the two contexts of being experienced as either pure or impure].

The argument may be summarized like this: As long as there appear completely pure bodies and fields of experience, as well as completely impure bodies and fields of experience, then, since all that is differentiated with reference to location and time are appearances of a single moment of the all-ground consciousness, [the achievement of pure appearance] is not in any way an achievement of primordial properties. Just as, for example, the characteristics of space are not established within space.[272] This is also an unmistaken proof.

The eight collections of consciousness, which are distinguished by means of their function, belong to the all-ground consciousness and they are hence not different from each other. Also, the distinction between the mind-stream of oneself and the mind-streams of others is made with reference to persons and not with reference to phenomena. Reasonings differ with regard to their scope, and the establishment of the appearances of delusion as valid is, with regard to appearance itself, not without fault. However, when an intelligent individual establishes [appearances as divine] in this way he will not be unable to establish that which is to be proven.

The Great[273] *Establishment of Appearances as Divine* was composed by Dharmabhadra.

May it be virtuous!

Comparative Edition of Establishing Appearances as Divine

FOUR EDITIONS of *Establishing Appearances as Divine* were available for this project.

One was purportedly discovered by the Nyingma master Khordong Tertrul Chimey Rigdzin ('Khor gdong gter sprul 'chi med rig 'dzin) (1922-2002) as part of an incomplete collection of Rongzom's writings he is said to have found at Shantiniketan in West Bengal.[274] This collection was published in Leh in 1974 by Tashigangpa under the title *Selected Writings* (*Gsung Thor bu*) *of Rongzom Chökyi Zangpo* in his *Smanrtsis shesrig spendzod* series (henceforth *CR*). *CR* itself is based on a handwritten manuscript by Chimey Rigdzin.[275] Generally, this version contains many omissions and spelling errors.

The second available edition of *Establishing Appearances as Divine* was published in 2001 and edited by Rinchen (Rin chen) and Sonam Lodro (Bsod nams blo gros) (henceforth *RS*). While *RS* lacks the omissions of *CR*, it bears witness to the creativity of the scribes (the archaic term *gzugs por* that Rongzom uses frequently throughout his writings has been exchanged with the nowadays more common term *gzu bor*).

Two other editions of *Establishing Appearances as Divine* were available for this project, one published in Sichuan 1999 (henceforth *S*), and the other in California in 1995 by the Yeshe De Project (henceforth *C*). These two resemble each other closely and, as they contain only a few typographical errors, I believe that these are the most reliable ones.

Besides these four copies, Kunzang Topgay reportedly discovered another incomplete print of Rongzom's writings, which he published in 1976 at Thimphu. This edition was not available for this project.[276]

All these editions of *Establishing Appearances as Divine* stem, according to Gene Smith, from a single manuscript from Nyide Gon (Nyi lde Dgon) in Lhadrag (Lha brag). This manuscript surfaced in the early twentieth century and was carved onto woodblocks[277] through the efforts of Mipham and probably Kathog Situ Chökyi Gyatso (Kah thog si tu chos kyi rgya mtsho) (1880-1923/25), as part of a two-volume edition of the collected works (*gsung bum*) of Rongzom, for which Mipham prepared an index (*dkar chag*).[278]

In comparing the four editions, no data suggestive of an alternative source for any of them was found. With its frequent spelling errors and omissions of whole sentences, *CR* is the edition that deviates most from the others, yet not sufficiently to suggest a distinct source.[279] Likewise, *CR* and *S* on two occasions agree in using the term *ka ba* instead of *lag pa* as found in *C* and *RS*, yet the otherwise overwhelming similarities between all four editions makes the conclusion that they are all based on the Nyide Gon manuscript compelling. When screening *CR* and *S* for other unique similarities I found only two occasions where the editions agree in applying a genitive particle instead of the instrumental particle that the text seems to demand. *C* and *RS* accord on a number of occasions in using the *pa* particle instead of *ba*. Once they both omit *ma* and elsewhere agree on choosing the future tense of the verb *'thob*. I hypothesize that while all four editions are based on the same relatively recent mother manuscript, the *RS* + *C* and the *CR* + *S* editions are based on two slightly different descendants of that manuscript.

The Tibetan text of *Establishing Appearances as Divine* included here follows *S* for the reason that this version appears to be the one most readily available to the modern reader.[280]

༄༅། །གསང་སྔགས་རྡོ་རྗེ་ཐེག་པའི་ཚུལ་ལས་སྣང་བ་ལྷར་བསྒྲུབ་པ་རོང་ཟོམ་ཆོས་བཟང་གིས་མཛད་པ་བཞུགས།།

༄༅། །གསང་སྔགས་རྡོ་རྗེ་ཐེག་པའི་ཚུལ་ལས་འཇིག་རྟེན་དང་འཇིག་རྟེན་ལས་འདས་པའི་ཆོས་ཐམས་ཅད་དབྱེར་མེད་པར་སྐུ་གསུང་ཐུགས་རྡོ་རྗེ་ལྷ་བུའི་དཀྱིལ་འཁོར་དུ། ཡེ་ནས་སངས་རྒྱས་པ་ཡིན་པས་ད་ལམ་གྱིས་སྒྲུབ་[1] པ་ལྟ་བུ་ནི་མ་ཡིན་ནོ། །ཞེས་འབྱུང་བ་ལ། འདིར་བརྒལ་བ། ད་ལྟར་འགྲོ་བ་རྣམས་ཀྱི་སྤྱོད་ཡུལ་དུ་སྣང་བའི་ཆོས་འདི་དག་ནི། ཇི་ལྟར་སྣང་བ་དེ་ལྟར་མ་ཡིན་ཏེ། འཁྲུལ་པ་ཡིན་པས། ཡེ་ནས་སངས་རྒྱས་པ་ནི་ཡིན་དུ་མི་རུང་ངོ་ཞེ་ན། འཁྲུལ་པ་ཡིན་དུ་ཟད་དེ། སེམས་ཅན་གྱི་འཁྲུལ་བ་[2] ལས་མ་གཏོགས་པའི་ཆོས་གཞན་ཅི་ཡང་བཞག་ཅིང་བསྟན་དུ་མེད་དེ། འཁྲུལ་སྣང་དུ་གྲགས་པའི་ཆོས་འདི་ཙམ་ཞེས་བྱ་བ་ཡིན་ནོ། །དེ་བས་ན་མུ་སྟེགས་ཅན་གྱིས་གང་ཟག་གི་བདག་རྟག་པར་ཡོད་བརྟགས་པར་དང་། བྱེ་བྲག་ཏུ་སྨྲ་བ་ཁ་ཅིག་གིས་གང་ཟག་དེ་མི་རྟག་པའི་མཚན་ཉིད་དུ་ཡོད་པར་འདོད་པ་དང་། བྱེ་བྲག་ཏུ་སྨྲ་བ་ཁ་ཅིག་དང་མདོ་སྡེ་པས་གང་ཟག་བཀག་སྟེ། དེས་སྟོང་པའི་ཕུང་པོ་ལ་སོགས་པའི་ཆོས་ཀྱི་མཚན་ཉིད་ཡོད་པར་འདོད་པ་དང་། རྣལ་འབྱོར་སྤྱོད་པ་བས་གཞན་གྱི་དབང་གི་མཚན་ཉིད་ལ་ཀུན་[3] བརྟགས་པས་སྟོང་པའི། སྟོང་པ་ཉིད་དང་བཅས་པའི་གཞན་དབང་ཡོད་པར་འདོད་པ་དང་། དབུ་མ་པས་དོན་དམ་པར་ཆོས་ཐམས་ཅད་ལ་ཡོད་པ་དང་མེད་པ་ལ་སོགས་ཏེ་

1 *CR* sgrubs
2 *CR* pa
3 *C* kun tu

མཐའ་ཐམས་ཅད་དང་བྲལ་ཏེ། སྤྲོས་པ་ཡོངས་སུ་བཅད་པའོ། །ཞེས་འདོད་པ་དང་། གསང་སྔགས་ཀྱི་ཚུལ་ལས་བདེན་པ་རྣམ་པ་གཉིས་དབྱེར་མེད་པ་དང་། གདོད་མ་ནས་སངས་རྒྱས་པ་ལ་སོགས་པ་རྣམས་འགྲོ་བ་རྣམས་ཀྱིས་མཐུན་པར་སྣང་བའི་མཚན་ཉིད་ལ་ལྟ་བ་སོ་སོར་འཛོག་ཅིང་རྩོད་པ་ཡིན་ཏེ། དེའི་ཕྱིར་ཆོས་ཅན་གཞན་ཞིག་ཡོད་པ་ནི་མ་ཡིན་ནོ། །དེ་བས་ན་སྣང་བའི་ཆོས་འདི་དག་ཐམས་ཅད་འཁྲུལ་བ་[1] ཡིན་དུ་ཟད་དེ། དེ་ཡང་འཁྲུལ་བ་[2] བསལ་ནས་མ་འཁྲུལ་པ་[3] ཞིག་བསྒྲུབ་ཏུ་མེད་དེ། འཁྲུལ་པ་ངོ་བོ་ཉིད་ཀྱིས་རྣམ་པར་དག་པས་སངས་རྒྱས་པ་ཡིན་ཏེ། དེ་བས་ན་ཆོས་ཐམས་ཅད་ཡེ་ནས་མངོན་པར་རྫོགས་པར་སངས་རྒྱས་པའོ། །དེ་བས་ན་མཚན་མ་སྣ་ཚོགས་སུ་སྣང་བའི་ཆོས་རྣམས་སྐུ་གསུང་ཐུགས་རྡོ་རྗེའི་དཀྱིལ་འཁོར་ཉིད་ཡིན་ཏེ། རྣམ་པར་དག་པའི་ངོ་བོ་ཉིད་ལས་མ་འདས་པ་དུས་གསུམ་གྱི་སངས་རྒྱས་ཉིད་དང་འདྲ་བའོ། །སེམས་ཅན་དང་སངས་རྒྱས་ཀྱི་ཁྱད་པར་ནི་ཆོས་ཀྱི་ངོ་བོ་ཉིད་ཀྱིས་ཕྱེ་བ་མ་ཡིན་ཏེ། རྨི་ལམ་གྱི་རྒྱུ་འབྲས་བུ་སོ་སོར་སྣང་བ་བཞིན་དུ། ཀུན་ཏུ་བཏགས་པའི་དབང་གིས་བློ་སོ་སོར་སྣང་བ་ཙམ་ལ་བཞག་པར་ཟད་དོ། །འདིར་དྲིས་པ། ལུང་ལས་དེ་ལྟར་གསུངས་ཀྱང་གཟུགས་པོར་[4] གསུངས་སམ། དགོངས་པ་དང་བཅས་པར་གསུངས་པ་ངེས་པ་མེད་པས་ཆོས་ངོ་བོ་ཉིད་ཀྱིས་དག་པ་ནི་གྲུབ་ཏུ་རུང་ན། ཆོས་ཅན་མཚན་མར་[5] སྣང་བ་འདི་ཉིད་ཀྱི་རང་བཞིན་ཡེ་ནས་སངས་རྒྱས་པ་ཡིན་པར་ནི་རིགས་པ་མ་ཡིན་ཏེ། དེ་ལྟ་ན་ནི་ཀུན་ནས་ཉོན་མོངས་པ་དང་འཁོར་བ་ཡང་གཏན་མེད་པར་འགྱུར་རོ། །དེ་[6] ལྟ་བུའི་གྲུབ་མཐའ་འགྲུབ་པར་འགྱུར་བའི་རིགས་པའང་མེད་དོ་ཞེ་ན། སེམས་ཅན་གྱི་སྤྱོད་ཡུལ་དུ་སྣང་

1 *CR, C* pa
2 *CR, C* pa
3 *CR* ba
4 *RS* gzu bor
5 *CR* instead of ra:ba
6 *S* da

བའི་དོན་ཚད་མར་བྱས་ནས་ཐོག་མ་མེད་པའི་དུས་ནས་རྟོག་པའི་བློ་འཁྲུལ་བས་[1] ཇི་ལྟར་སྣང་བ་དེ་ལྟར་སྒྲུབ་པ་དང་། དགག་པ་བྱས་པའི་རྟོག་གེ་ནི་ཟབ་ཅིང་རྒྱ་ཆེ་བའི་དོན་ལ་བསྒྲུབ་པར་ནུས་པ་མ་ཡིན་མོད་ཀྱི་འོན་ཀྱང་ཆོས་ཉིད་བསམ་གྱིས་མི་ཁྱབ་པ་ཡིན་པས། སོ་སོར་རྟོག་པའི་ཤེས་རབ་ཀྱིས་རྟོགས་པའི་ཐབས་མེད་པ་ཡང་མ་ཡིན་ཏེ། དེ་བས་ན་དད་པ་ཙམ་གྱིས་འཇུག་པར་སྤྱོ་བ་རྣམས་ལུང་[2] དང་མན་ངག་ཉིད་ཚད་མར་བྱས་ཏེ། ཡིད་ཆེས་པའི་བློ་ཞུགས་ན་ཉེས་[3] པ་འགའ་ཡང་མེད་དོ། །གང་ཞིག་རིགས་པས་[4] མ་གྲུབ་ན་འཇུག་པར་མི་འགྱུར་རོ་ཞེ་ན། དེ་དག་ལ་[5] ཡང་མཐུན་པར་བསྒྲུབ་[6] པར་བྱའོ། །དེ་ལ་ཆོས་དེ་དག་སྐུ་གསུང་ཐུགས་རྡོ་རྗེའི་དཀྱིལ་འཁོར་དུ་སངས་རྒྱས་པ་ལ། ཆོས་ཉིད་ཀྱི་རིགས་པས་གྲུབ་སྟེ། ཇི་ལྟར་མདོ་ལས། གཟུགས་རང་བཞིན་གྱིས་སྟོང་པ་སྟེ། ཅིའི་ཕྱིར་ཞེ་ན། དེའི་རང་བཞིན་དེ་ཡིན་པའི་ཕྱིར་རོ། །ཞེས་གསུངས་ཏེ། ཆོས་ཐམས་ཅད་ཆོས་ཉིད་ཀྱིས་དག་པས། མ་དག་པའི་ཆོས་ཙུང་ཟད་ཀྱང་མེད་པ་[7] ཆོས་རྣམས་ཀྱི་ཆོས་ཉིད་པས། ལུས་ངག་ཡིད་གསུམ་ཡང་རྣམ་པར་དག་པ་རང་གི་ཆོས་ཉིད་ཡིན་ཏེ། རྣམ་པར་དག་པ་ནི་སངས་རྒྱས་པའོ། །དེས་ན་རྣམ་པར་དག་པས་ཕྱེ་བའི་ལུས་ངག་ཡིད་ནི་དབྱེར་མེད་ཅིང་སྤྲོས་པ་མེད་པ་དང་། རྫོགས་པར་ཁྱབ་པའི་ཕྱིར་སྐུ་གསུང་ཐུགས་རྡོ་རྗེའི་དཀྱིལ་འཁོར་ཉིད་ཡིན་པར་རིགས་པར་བྱའོ། །དེ་ལྟར་ཆོས་ཉིད་ཀྱི་རིགས་པས་གྲུབ་ན་རིགས་པ་ལྷག་མ་གསུམ་བསྒྲུབ་མི་དགོས་ཏེ། རིགས་པ་གསུམ་པའི་རྟེན་དེ་ཡིན་པའི་ཕྱིར་དང་དེ་གཙོ་བོ་ཡིན་པའི་ཕྱིར་རོ། །ཡང་དྲིས་པ། ཆོས་ཉིད་དེ་

1 *CR, C* pas
2 *CR* 2 times lung
3 *CR* te sa
4 *CR* las
5 *CR* om. la
6 *CR* sgrub
7 *RS* par

ནི་བདག་ཅག་ལ་མ་གྲུབ་པས། རིགས་པ་གཞན་གྱིས་སྒྲུབ་དགོས་སོ་ཞེ་ན། དེ་ཡང་བསྒྲུབ་པར་བྱ་སྟེ། དེ་ལ་བྱ་བ་བྱེད་པའི་རིགས་པ་ནི། དངོས་པོ་རྣམས་འབྲས་བུའི་སྒོ་ནས་རྒྱུ་ཤེས་པར་བྱེད་པ་སྟེ། ཇི་ལྟར་སྨན་དང་དུག་གིས་འཚོ་བ་དང་འཆི་བའི་བྱ་བ་བྱེད་པ་དམིགས་པས། བྱ་བའི་སྒོ་ནས་བྱེད་པ་ཤེས་པ་ཡིན་པ་བཞིན། གང་གིས[1] སྐུ་གསུང་ཐུགས་རྡོ་རྗེའི་དཀྱིལ་འཁོར་དུ་བསྒོམས་པས། ལུས་དང་ངག་དང་ཡིད་དག་པའི་དངོས་གྲུབ་ཐོབ་པར་དམིགས་པའི་ཕྱིར། སྣང་བའི་ཆོས་རྣམས་སྐུ་གསུང་ཐུགས་རྡོ་རྗེའི་ངོ་བོ་ཉིད་དང་མཐུ་ཅན་དུ་བྱ་བ་བྱེད་པའི་རིགས་པས་གྲུབ་པ་ཡིན་ནོ། །དངོས་པོའི་ནུས་པ་ལ་མ་ལྟོས་པར་བསྒྲུབ་པ་ཙམ་གྱིས་འགྲུབ་པ་ཡང་མ་ཡིན་ཏེ། ཇི་ལྟར་ནོར་བུ་རིན་པོ་ཆེ་སྟར་ལོངས་སྤྱོད་ཀྱི་རྐྱེན་དུ་མ་སྤྱད་པ་ཞིག་གང་ཞིག་གིས་རྙེད་པ་ལས། དེས་རིན་པོ་ཆེ་ངོ་མ་ཤེས་ཏེ། ནོར་བུ་ཕལ་པར་བཞག་ནས་ཡོན་ཏན་མཐོང་བ་ཡང་མེད་པ་ལས། ཕྱིས་ནོར་བུའི་རིགས་ཤེས་པས་བསྟན་ཏེ། དེས་བྱི་དོར་བྱས་ཤིང་མཆོད་པ་ལས། གདོད་ནོར་བུ་དེ་ལས་ཡོན་ཏན་ཁྱད་པར་ཅན་འབྱུང་སྟེ། བྱ་བ་ཁྱད་པར་ཅན་དམིགས་པས་རིན་པོ་ཆེ་ཉིད་དུ་ངེས་པ་ལྟར། ཐ་མལ་པའི་ལུས་དང་ངག་དང་ཡིད་ཀྱང་ལྷར[2] མ་ཤེས་ཤིང་མ་བཀུར་ན། ཡོན་ཏན་མི་དམིགས་ཏེ། ཤེས་ཤིང་བཀུར་བས་གཞི་དེ་ཉིད་ལས་ཡོན་ཏན་དམིགས་པའི་ཕྱིར་རོ། །ལྟོས་པའི་རིགས་པས་ཀྱང་གྲུབ་སྟེ། དེ་ལ་ལྟོས་པའི་རིགས་པ་ནི། དངོས་པོ་རྣམས་རྒྱུས་འབྲས་བུ་རྟོགས་པར་བྱེད་པ་སྟེ། དེ་ལ་སྐྱེ་བ་གྲུབ་པར་བྱེད་པ། ས་བོན་ལ་ལྟོས་ནས་མྱུ་གུ་གྲུབ་པར་བྱེད་པའམ། ཐ་སྙད་སྒྲུབ་པར་བྱེད་པ། ངན་པ་ལ་ལྟོས་ནས་བཟང་པོའི་ཐ་སྙད་གྲུབ་པར་བྱེད་པ་བཞིན། སྣང་བའི་ཆོས་ཐམས་ཅད་ནི་སེམས་ཉིད་ཀྱི་རྣམ་པར་སྣང་བ་སྟེ། དེ་བས་ན་སེམས་ཀྱི་རྒྱུ་ལ་ལྟོས་ནས་འབྲས་བུ་དག་པ་དང་མ་དག་པ་ཐམས་ཅད་སྐྱེ་བ་འགྲུབ་པར་བྱེད་པ་ཡིན་པས།

1 *S, CR* gi
2 *CR* ltar

དེའི་ཕྱིར་དག་པའི་སྤྱོད་ཡུལ་དང་མ་དག་པའི་སྤྱོད་ཡུལ་ཐམས་ཅད་བག་ཆགས་ཀྱིས་བསྐྱེད་པའི་སེམས་ཀྱི་འབྲས་བུ་ཡིན་པས་གཉི་ག་ཡང་མཚན་ཉིད་པར་གྲུབ་པ་ཡིན་ནོ། །དེ་གཉིས་ལ་གང་ཞིག་འཁྲུལ་པའམ་[1] མ་འཁྲུལ་པར་[2] བཞག་པ་ནི། ལྟོས་པའི་རིགས་[3] པས་གྲུབ་སྟེ། དེའི་ཕྱིར་དག་པའི་སྤྱོད་ཡུལ་ནི་སྣང་བ་མཚན་ཉིད་ཡིན་[4] པར་ངེས་པར་རྟོགས་པར་བྱའོ། །དེ་ལྟར་རིགས་པ་རྣམ་པ་གསུམ་གྱིས་གྲུབ་ན། འཐད་པ་བསྒྲུབ་པའི་རིགས་པས་སྒྲུབ་མི་དགོས་ཏེ། ཇི་ལྟར་ཆོས་ཉིད་དང་རྒྱུ་དང་འབྲས་བུ་མ་གཏོགས་པའི་གཏན་ཚིགས་མངོན་སུམ་དང་རྗེས་སུ་དཔག་པ་ལ་ཡང་མེད་པའི་ཕྱིར་རོ༎

འོ་ན་འཐད་པ་སྒྲུབ་པ་ཅི་ལ་དགོས་ཤེ་ན། དེ་ནི་དབང་པོ་དམན་པ་རྣམས་ལ་རིགས་པ་ཉིད་སྟོན་ལ་བསྒྲུབས་ཏེ། དེས་དོན་[5] ལ་འཇལ་བར་བྱེད་དགོས་པའི་ཕྱིར། ཆོས་ཅན་དང་བསྒྲུབ་བྱ་དང་དཔེ་སྦྱར་བ་དང་། ཁྱབ་པ་ལྡོག་པ་ངེས་པས། བསྒྲུབ་དགོས་པ་རྣམས་ཀྱི་ཕྱིར་ཡིན་ནོ། །ཡང་དྲིས་པ། གང་ཟག་ཁ་ཅིག་ནི་དེ་ཙམ་གྱིས་འགྲུབ་པར་འགྱུར་ན། ཁ་ཅིག་ལ་འཐད་པ་སྒྲུབ་པའི་རིགས་པ་ཉིད་ཀྱིས་མ་གྲུབ་ན།

ཡིད་ཆེས་པར་མི་འགྱུར་བས། དེ་བསྒྲུབ་པར་གྱིས་ཤིག[6] སྨྲས་པ། དང་པོར་གཉིས་[7] ག་ལ་གྲུབ་པའི་ལུང་གིས་བསྒྲུབ་པར་བྱ་སྟེ། ཡེ་ཤེས་སྣང་བ་རྒྱན་གྱི་མདོ་ལས། རྟག་ཏུ་སྐྱེ་མེད་ཆོས་ནི་དེ་བཞིན་གཤེགས། །ཆོས་རྣམས་ཐམས་ཅད་བདེ་བར་གཤེགས་དང་འདྲ། །བྱིས་པའི་བློ་ཅན་མཚན་མར་འཛིན་པ་དག །འཇིག་རྟེན་དག་ན་མེད་པའི་ཆོས་ལ་སྤྱོད། །ཅེས་གསུངས་ཏེ། དེ་ལ་རྟག་ཏུ་སྐྱེ་མེད་ཆོས་ནི་དེ་བཞིན་གཤེགས་ཞེས་བྱ་བ་ནི་

1 *CR* ba'am
2 *CR* bar
3 *S* rig
4 *CR* len
5 *CR* om. don
6 *CR* /
7 *RS* gnyi

གཏན་ཚིགས་སོ། །ཆོས་རྣམས་ཐམས་ཅད་ཅེས་བྱ་བ་ནི་ཆོས་ཅན་ནོ། །བདེ་བར་གཤེགས་པ་དང་འདྲ་ཞེས་བྱ་བ་ནི་དཔེའོ། །བསྒྲུབ་བྱ་ནི་ཆོས་ཐམས་ཅད་དེ་བཞིན་གཤེགས་པ་ཡིན་པར་བསྒྲུབ་པར་བྱ་བ་ཡིན་པའོ། །འོ་ན་མངོན་སུམ་གྱི་ཚད་མས་[1] གནོད་ཅེ་ན། བྱིས་པའི་བློ་ཅན་མཚན་མར་འཛིན་པ་དག །འཇིག་རྟེན་དག་ན་མེད་པའི་ཆོས་ལ་སྤྱོད། ཅེས་གསུངས་ཏེ། ཇི་ལྟར་བརྡའ་ལ་མ་བྱུང་བའི་བྱིས་པ་དག་རབ་རིབ་གྱི་སྒྲ་ཤད་ལ་འཛིན་པ་དང་། མགལ་མེའི་འཁོར་ལོ་ལ་ལོངས་སྤྱོད་ཅིང་དགའ་བ་སྐྱེ་བ་ལྟར་བྱིས་པ་སོ་སོའི་སྐྱེ་བོ་རྣམས་འཁྲུལ་པའི་ཤེས་པས་བརྟགས་[2]པའི་སྤྱོད་ཡུལ་མཚན་མར་འཛིན་པའི་ལོངས་སྤྱོད་པ་ནི་མེད་པའི་ཆོས་ལ་ལོངས་སྤྱོད་པར་ཟད་དོ། །དེ་བས་ན་འདི་ལྟར་བསྒྲུབ་པ་ཡིན་ཏེ། ཆོས་ཐམས་ཅད་ནི་དེ་བཞིན་གཤེགས་པ་ཡིན་ཏེ། རྟག་ཏུ་སྐྱེ་བ་མེད་པའི་ཆོས་དེ་དེ་བཞིན་གཤེགས་པ་ཡིན་པའི་ཕྱིར། དཔེར་ན་དུས་གསུམ་གྱི་བདེ་བར་གཤེགས་པ་དང་འདྲའོ། །ཇི་ལྟར་འདྲ་ཞེ་ན་བདེ་བར་གཤེགས་པ་ནི་ལུས་དང་ངག་དང་ཡིད་ཀྱིས་ཕྱེ་བ་མ་ཡིན་ཏེ། ཆོས་ཉིད་ཀྱིས་ཕྱེ་བ་ཡིན་ཏེ།[3] འདི་ལྟར་འདུས་མ་བྱས་ཀྱིས་ཕྱེ་བ་ནི་འཕགས་པའི་གང་ཟག་གོ །ཞེས་བརྗོད་པ་ཡིན་ནོ། །དེ་བཞིན་འཕགས་པ་རྣམས་འདུས་མ་བྱས་ཐོབ་པས་འཕགས་པ་ཉིད་ཐོབ་པ་[4]བཞིན། ཆོས་ཐམས་ཅད་འདུས་མ་བྱས་པའི་རང་བཞིན་ཐོབ་པས་དེ་བཞིན་གཤེགས་པ་ཡིན་ནོ། །མཚན་མའི་སྤྱོད་ཡུལ་ནི་དེ་ལྟ་མ་ཡིན་[5]ཏེ། དེ་ལྟར་མེད་བཞིན་དུ་སྤྱོད་པར་འདོད་པ་རྣམས་མེད་པའི་ཆོས་ལ་སྤྱོད་དུ་ཟད་དོ། །འོ་ན་ངོ་བོ་ཉིད་ཀྱིས་སངས་རྒྱས་པའི་བདག་ཉིད་དུ་གྲུབ་ན། སྣང་བ་ཙམ་གྱི་ངོར་སྐུ་གསུང་ཐུགས་རྡོ་རྗེའི་དཀྱིལ་འཁོར་དུ་གྲུབ་པའི་

1 *CR* tshad mas ci gnod
2 *CR* btags
3 *CR* om. chos nyid kyis phye ba yin
4 *CR* om. thob pa
5 *CR* om. yin

འཐད་པ་སྒྲུབ་པའི་རིགས་པ་ཅི་ཡོད་ཅེ་ན། དེ་ཡང་བསྒྲུབ་པར་བྱ་སྟེ་དེ་ལ་ཡང་ཅིག་ཅར་བསྒྲུབ་པར་བྱ་བའམ། འོན་ཏེ་རིམ་གྱིས་ཀྱང་བསྒྲུབ་པར་བྱ་སྟེ། དེ་ལྟར་རང་གི་སྣང་བ་ལ་ཞེན་པ་ཆུང་བ་རྣམས་ནི་ཅིག་ཆར་བསྒྲུབ་པས་ཁོང་དུ་ཆུད་[1] པར་འགྱུར་ཏེ། དེ་ལ་དང་པོ་ཉིད་དུ་དཔེ་བསྒྲུབ་པར་བྱའོ། །ཇི་ལྟར་ཡི་དྭགས་རྣམས་ཀྱིས་ཆུ་ཀླུང་ལ་རྣག་ཏུ་མཐོང་བ་ལས། ཁ་ཅིག་གིས་མི་རྣམས་ཀྱིས་ཆུར་[2] མཐོང་བ་ཡང་ཐོས་ཏེ། དེ་ལ་ལ་ལ་ནི། རྣག་གི་དངོས་པོའི་མཚན་ཉིད་ཡིན་ཏེ། ཆུ་ནི་ཀུན་བརྟགས་པའི་གཟུགས་སུ་འདོད་ལ། ཁ་ཅིག་གིས་[3] ནི་[4] རྣག་ནི་སྣང་བ་མ་དག་པ་ཡིན་པས་མི་རྣམས་ཀྱིས་མཐོང་བ་བཞིན་དུ་ཆུ་ཉིད་མཚན་ཉིད་པར་འདོད་པ་ལས། དེས་སྨྲས་པ། གྲོགས་པོ་དག་བདག་ཅག་ལྟ་བུའི་ཡི་དྭགས་[5] རྣམས་ལ་མཐུན་པར་སྣང་བའི་རྣག་གིས་གང་བའི་ཆུ་ཀླུང་འདི་ནི། མི་རྣམས་ཀྱིས་མཐོང་བ་བཞིན་དུ་[6] ཆུ་ཀླུང་ཉིད་ཡིན་ཏེ། ཆུ་ལ་སྤྱོད་པར་དབང་བ་རྣམས་ཀྱིས་བསྔོས་ཏེ་བྱིན་ན་ཡི་དྭགས་རྣམས་ལ་ཡང་ཆུ་ཉིད་དུ་སྣང་ཞིང་ལོངས་སྤྱོད་དུ་ཡོད་པའི་ཕྱིར་[7] བདག་ཅག་ཉིད་ཀྱིས་སྔོན་ཆད་སྐབས་སྐབས་སུ་ཐོབ་པའི་ཆུ་བཞིན་ནོ། །ཞེས་འབྲེལ་བ་བསྒྲུབ་ན་འདི་ནི་སྐྱོན་མེད་པར་འབྲེལ་བ་འགྲུབ་བོ། །ཡང་གང་[8] ཆུ་ལ་དབང་བ་རྣམས་ཀྱིས་བསྔོས་ཏེ་བྱིན་ན། ཆུ་ཉིད་ལོངས་སྤྱོད་[9] དུ་ཡོད་པ་དེ་ཐམས་ཅད་ནི་ཆུ་ཉིད་ཡིན་ཏེ། བདག་ཅག་གིས་ཐོས་ཐོས་པའི་ཆུ་ལྟ་བུའོ། །འདི་ཡང་ཆུ་ལ་སྤྱོད་པར་དབང་བ་རྣམས་ཀྱིས་བསྔོས་ཏེ་བྱིན་ན་ཆུ་ཉིད་ལ་ལོངས་སྤྱོད་དུ

1 *CR* chung
2 *CR* chud
3 *CR* om. gis
4 *RS* om. ni
5 *CR* ngags
6 *CR* nu
7 *RS* /
8 *CR* gad
9 *CR* spyad

ཡོད་པའོ་ཞེས་ཁྲབ་པ་[1] ངེས་པར་གྲུབ་པ་བཞིན་མི་རྣམས་ལ་མཐུན་པར་སྣང་བའི་ལུས་དང་ལོངས་སྤྱོད་དུ་སྣང་བ་འདི་དག་ལ། ཁ་ཅིག་གིས་ཡོངས་སུ་དག་པའི་གང་ཟག་རྣམས་ཀྱིས་ལྷའི་དཀྱིལ་འཁོར་དུ་མཐོང་བ་དང་། གསང་སྔགས་ཀྱི་ཚུལ་ལས་ལྷའི་དཀྱིལ་འཁོར་ཉིད་ཡིན་པར་སྟོན་པའང་ཐོས་ཏེ། དེ་ལས་ལ་ལ་ནི་ཐ་མལ་པའི་ལུས་དང་ལོངས་སྤྱོད་དུ་སྣང་བ་ནི་དངོས་པོའི་མཚན་ཉིད་དེ། ལྷར་མཐོང་བ་ནི་ཀུན་བརྟགས་པ་ལ་སོགས་པར་འདོད་པ་ལ། ཁ་ཅིག་ནི་ཐ་མལ་པའི་ལུས་དང་ལོངས་སྤྱོད་[2] ནི་སྣང་བ་མ་དག་པ་ཡིན་པས། གང་ཟག་དག་པ་རྣམས་ཀྱིས་མཐོང་བ་དང་། གསང་སྔགས་ཀྱི་ཚུལ་ལས་གྲགས་པ་བཞིན་དུ། ལྷ་ཉིད་དངོས་པོ་རྣམས་ཀྱི་མཚན་ཉིད་ཡིན་པར་འདོད་པ་ལས། ངེས་སླུས་པ། གྲོགས་པོ་དག་བདག་ཅག་ལྷ་བུ་མི་རྣམས་ལ་མཐུན་པར་སྣང་བའི་ཐ་མལ་པའི་ལུས་དང་ལོངས་སྤྱོད་ཡུལ་དུ་སྣང་བ་འདི་ནི། གང་ཟག་དག་པ་རྣམས་ཀྱིས་མཐོང་བ་བཞིན་དུ་ལྷའི་དཀྱིལ་འཁོར་ཉིད་ཡིན་ཏེ། དག་པའི་སྤྱོད་ཡུལ་ལ་སྤྱོད་པར་དབང་བ་རྣམས་ཀྱིས་དངོས་གྲུབ་བྱིན་ན་མི་རྣམས་ལ་ཡང་སྤྱོད་ཡུལ་འདི་དག་ལྷ་ཉིད་དུ་སྣང་ཞིང་ལོངས་སྤྱོད་དུ་ཡོད་པའི་ཕྱིར་བདག་ཅག་ལྷ་བུའི་མི་ལས་སྔོན་ཅད་[3] སྐབས་སྐབས་སུ་དངོས་གྲུབ་ཐོབ་པ་བྱུང་[4] བ་རྣམས་ཀྱིས་ལྷའི་སྤྱོད་ཡུལ་ཐོབ་པ་བཞིན་ནོ།། ཞེས་འབྲེལ་བ་བསྒྲུབས་ན་འདི་ནི་སྐྱོན་མེད་པར་གྲུབ་པའོ། །ཡང་གང་དག་པའི་སྤྱོད་ཡུལ་ལ་དབང་བ་རྣམས་ཀྱིས་དངོས་གྲུབ་བྱིན་ན་ལྷ་ཉིད་ཀྱི་སྤྱོད་ཡུལ་ལ་ལོངས་སྤྱོད་དུ་ཡོད་པ་དེ་ཐམས་ཅད་ལྷ་ཉིད་ཡིན་ཏེ། དངོས་གྲུབ་ཅན་གྱིས་ཐོབ་པའི་ལྷའི་སྤྱོད་ཡུལ་ལྷ་བུའོ། །ཐ་མལ་པའི་སྤྱོད་ཡུལ་འདི་ཡང་། ཡོངས་སུ་དག་པའི་སྤྱོད་ཡུལ་ལ་སྤྱོད་

1 *RS* par
2 *CR* om. snang ba ni dngos po'i mtshan nyid de/ lhar mthong ba ni kun brtags pa la sogs par 'dod pa la/ kha cig ni tha mal pa'i lus dang longs spyod
3 *RS* chad
4 *CR* 'byung ba

པར་དབང་བ་རྣམས་ཀྱིས་དངོས་གྲུབ་བྱིན་ན་ལྷའི་སྤྱོད་ཡུལ་ལ་ལོངས་སྤྱོད་དུ་ཡོད་པའོ། །ཞེས་སྒྲུབ་པ་འདི་ནི་ཁྱབ་པ་ངེས་པར་གྲུབ་པའོ། །མངོན་སུམ་གྱིས་ཀྱང་གནོད་པ་མ་ཡིན་ཏེ། ལས་ཀྱི་སྒྲིབ་པས་བསྒྲིབས་པ་ཡིན་པའི་ཕྱིར། དཔེར་ན་སྔོན་འཛམ་བུའི་གླིང་གི་བུད་མེད་དབུལ་མོ་ཞིག་ལ་ལྷ་རྣམས་ཀྱིས་[1] སྙིང་རྗེ་སྐྱེས་ནས་གསེར་བྱིན་པ་ལས་སོལ་བར་སོང་བ་བཞིན་ནོ། །ལས་དང་སྙིང་རྗེས་འབྲེལ་པ་ཡོད་པ་རྣམས་ལ་ནི། རིམ་པ་བཞིན་སྣང་བ་འབྱུང་སྟེ། འདི་ལྟར་དབུལ་མོ་དེ་ཉིད་ལ་མི་ལྷས་བྱིན་པའི་གསེར་ཅུང་ཟད་ཙམ་སྣང་བར་ནུས་ནས་ལོངས་སྤྱོད་ཅུང་ཟད་ཙམ་སྦྱར་བ་[2] བཞིན་ནོ། །གང་དག་རང་གི་སྣང་བ་ལ་ཤིན་ཏུ་མངོན་པར་ཞེན་པ་[3] རྣམས་ནི་དང་པོ་རང་གི་སྣང་བ་བདེན་པར་མ་བསྒྲུབ་ན། གཞི་ཉིད་ལ་འཇུག་པར་མི་འགྱུར་བས། དེ་ལྟ་བུ་ལ་ཐོག་མར་རང་གི་སྣང་བ་ཡང་བསྒྲུབས་ནས། དེ་ནས་གྲུབ་མཐའ་ཁྱད་པར་ཅན་ལ་རིམ་གྱིས་[4] གཞུགས་པར་བྱའོ། །དེ་ལྟ་བུའི་ཚུལ་ནི་འདི་ཡིན་ཏེ། དཔེར་ན་ཡི་དྭགས་གཉིས་སྟེ་མ་བཞིན་དུ་གྲུབ་མཐའ་མི་མཐུན་པ་ལས་གཅིག་གིས་སླུས་པ། བདག་ཅག་ལྟ་བུ་ལ་མཐུན་པར་སྣང་བའི་རྣག་གི་ཀླུང་འདི་ནི་རྣག་གི་མཚན་ཉིད་འབའ་ཞིག་ཏུ་མ་ཟད་ཀྱི་ཆུའི་མཚན་ཉིད་ཀྱང་ཡིན་ཏེ། སེམས་ཀྱི་རྣམ་པ་སྣང་བའི་ཕྱིར། བསྒོས་ནས་ཐོབ་པའི་ཆུ་དང་རྣག་ཏུ་སྣང་བ་འདི་ཉིད་བཞིན་ནོ། །ཞེས་བྱ་བ་དང་། ཡང་གང་སེམས་ཀྱི་རྣམ་པ་ཡིན་པ་དེ་ནི། མཚན་ཉིད་ཐམས་ཅད་དུ་སྣང་བ་ཡིན་ཏེ། བསྒོས་ནས་ཐོབ་པའི་ཆུ་དང་ཐ་མལ་པས་རྣག་ཏུ་སྣང་བ་འགའ་ཞིག་བཞིན་ནོ། །རྣག་གིས་གང་བའི་ཀླུང་ཆེན་པོ་འདི་ཡང་སེམས་ཀྱི་རྣམ་པ་སྣང་བའོ། །རྣམ་པ་ཡང་ཐ་དད་པ་མ་ཡིན་ཏེ། གཤེར་བ་མཐུན་སྣང་བར་མཐུན་པའི་ཕྱིར་རྣག་ཏུ་སྣང་བ་ཉིད་བཞིན་ནོ། །ཞེས་བསྒྲུབས་ན།

1 *CR* kyi
2 *CR* instead of sbyar ba: snang ba
3 *CR* two times zhen pa
4 *CR* kyi

སེམས་སྣང་བར་འདོད་པའི་གང་ཟག་རྣམས་ལ་རིགས་པ་འདི་གྲུབ་པ་ཡིན་ནོ། །དེ་ལྟར་དང་པོ་མཚུངས་པར་བསྒྲུབས་ནས། དེ་ནས་རྣག་གི་མཚན་ཉིད་དགག་པར་བྱ་སྟེ། འདི་ལྟར་སྣང་བ་འདི་གཉིས་ཀ་[1] ཡང་སེམས་ཀྱི་རྣམ་པ་སྣང་བ་ཡིན་པར་མཚུངས་མོད་ཀྱི་རྣག་ནི་སྣང་བ་མ་དག་པ་ཡིན་པའི་ཕྱིར། འཁྲུལ་པ་ཡིན་ལ། ཆུ་ནི་སྣང་བ་དག་པ་ཡིན་པའི་ཕྱིར་མ་འཁྲུལ་བའོ། །འདི་ལྟར་གང་འཁྲུལ་པ་དེ་ནི་མ་དག་པ་ཡིན་ལ། མ་དག་པ་དེ་ནི་འཁྲུལ་པ་[2] སྟེ། འདི་ནི་ཁྱབ་པ་མཚུངས་པའོ། །དེ་བཞིན་དུ་དག་པ་དང་མ་འཁྲུལ་བ་ལ་ཡང་བལྟ་བར་བྱ་སྟེ། དེ་བས་ན་ཁྱབ་པ་ངེས་པའི་གཏན་ཚིགས་འདི་ཉིད་ཀྱིས། རྣག་ནི་སྣང་བ་འཁྲུལ་བའོ[3]། །འཁྲུལ་བའི་[4] སྣང་བའོ[5]། །ཆུ་ནི་མ་འཁྲུལ་བའོ[6]། །མ་འཁྲུལ་བའི་[7] སྣང་བའོ། །དེ་བཞིན་དུ་[8] ཆོས་ཐམས་ཅད་སྒྱུ་མ་ཙམ་དུ་སྣང་བའི་ངོར་ཡང་འགྲོ་བ་ཕལ་པ་ལ་སྣང་བ་ལྟར། ལུས་དང་ངག་དང་ཡིད་ཀྱིས་བསྡུས་པའི་ལུས་དང་སྤྱོད་ཡུལ་དུ་སྣང་བ་འདི་དག་སྡུག་བསྔལ་གྱི་རང་བཞིན། ཉོན་མོངས་པ་སྐྱེ་བའི་གནས་ཀྱི་མཚན་ཉིད་ཁོ་ན་མ་ཡིན་ཏེ། གང་ཟག་དག་པ་རྣམས་ལ་སྣང་བ་བཞིན་དུ། སྐུ་གསུང་ཐུགས་རྡོ་རྗེས་[9] བསྡུས་པ་ཞིང་དང་སྤྱོད་ཡུལ་ཡོངས་སུ་དག་པའི་བདག་ཉིད་དུ་སངས་རྒྱས་པའི་མཚན་ཉིད་ཀྱང་ཡིན་ཏེ། སེམས་ཀྱི་རྣམ་པ་སྣང་བ་ཡིན་པའི་ཕྱིར། དངོས་གྲུབ་དམ་པ་ཐོབ་པ་རྣམས་ལ་ལྟར་སྣང་བ་དང་། ཐ་མལ་པ་ལ་བུམ་པ་དང་ཀ་བ་ལ་སོགས་པར་སྣང་བ་བཞིན་ནོ། །ཞེས་བྱ་བ་དང་། ཡང་གང་དང་གང་

1 *CR* instead of gnyis ka: mtshungs pa
2 *CR* ba
3 *RS* pa'o
4 *RS* pa'i
5 *CR* om. 'khrul ba'i snang ba'o
6 *CR, RS, C* pa'o
7 *CR, RS, C* pa'i
8 *CR* om. du
9 *CR* rdo rje'i

སེམས་ཀྱི་རྣམ་པ་ཡིན་པ་དེ་དང་དེ་ཐམས་ཅད་ནི་མཚན་ཉིད་ཐམས་ཅད་དུ་སྣང་བ་ཡིན་ཏེ། ཁ་ཅིག་ལ་ལྟར་སྣང་བ་དང་ཁ་ཅིག་ལ་ཀ་བ་[1]ལ་སོགས་པར་སྣང་བ་བཞིན་ནོ། །ཐ་མལ་པ་ལ་སྣང་བའི་ལུས་དང་གནས་དང་ལོངས་སྤྱོད་ཡུལ་དུ་སྣང་བ་འདི་ཡང་[2]སེམས་ཀྱི་རྣམ་པ་སྣང་བའོ། །རྣམ་པ་ཡང་ཐ་དད་པ་མ་ཡིན་ཏེ། ལུས་དང་ངག་དང་ཡིད་ཀྱིས་བསྡུས་པའི་ལུས་དང་གནས་དང་སྤྱོད་ཡུལ་སྣང་བ་མཐུན་པའི་ཕྱིར་རོ། །ཀ་བ་ལ་སོགས་པར་སྣང་བ་ཉིད་བཞིན་ནོ་ཞེས་བསྒྲུབས་ན། སེམས་སྣང་བར་འདོད་པའི་གང་ཟག་རྣམས་ལ་རིགས་པ་འདི་གྲུབ་པ་ཡིན་ནོ། །དེ་ལྟར་དང་པོ་མཚུངས་པར་གྲུབ་ནས། དེ་ནས་སྡུག་བསྔལ་གྱི་མཚན་ཉིད་དགག་[3]པར་བྱ་སྟེ། སྣང་བ་འདི་གཉིས་ཀ་[4]ཡང་སེམས་ཀྱི་རྣམ་པ་སྣང་བ་ཡིན་པར་མཚུངས་མོད་ཀྱི། སྡུག་བསྔལ་དང་སྡུག་བསྔལ་གྱི་གནས་སུ་སྣང་བ་ནི། སྣང་བ་མ་དག་པ་ཡིན་པའི་ཕྱིར་འཁྲུལ་[5]བ་[6]ཡིན་ལ། ཐར་པ་དང་ཐར་པའི་གནས་སུ་སྣང་བ་ནི་དག་པའི་ཕྱིར་མ་འཁྲུལ་བ་[7]སྟེ། གང་འཁྲུལ་བ་[8]དེ་ནི་མ་དག་པ་ཡིན་ལ། མ་དག་པ་དེ་ནི་འཁྲུལ་བ་[9]སྟེ། འདི་ནི་ཁྱབ་པ་མཚུངས་པའོ། །དེ་བཞིན་དུ་དག་པ་དང་མ་འཁྲུལ་བ་[10]ལ་ཡང་བལྟ་བར་བྱའོ། །དེ་བས་ན་ཁྱབ་པ་ངེས་པའི་གཏན་ཚིགས་འདི་ཉིད་ཀྱིས་ཐ་མལ་པར་སྣང་བ་ནི་སྣང་བ་འཁྲུལ་བའོ[11]། །འཁྲུལ་

1 *RS, C* instead of ka ba: lag pa
2 *RS* /
3 *CR* dag
4 *CR* ga
5 *CR* mthul
6 *CR, RS, C* pa
7 *CR, RS, C* pa
8 *CR, RS, C* pa
9 *CR, RS, C* pa
10 *CR* pa
11 *CR, C* pa'o

བའི་[1]སྣང་བའོ། །ལྷ་ནི་སྣང་བ་མ་འཁྲུལ་བའོ་[2]། །མ་འཁྲུལ་པའི་[3]སྣང་བའོ། །ཞེས་ངེས་པར་རྟོགས་པར་བྱའོ།། །[4]དེ་ལ་རྣམ་པ་ཡང་ཐ་དད་མ་ཡིན་ཞེས་བྱ་བ་འདི་ཡང་ཅུང་ཟད་བཤད་པར་བྱ་སྟེ། གང་ཟག་ཁ་ཅིག་གིས་བཏགས་པ་བུམ་པ་དང་ཀ་བ་ལ་སོགས་པ་ལ་ལྷར་བསྒོམས་ན་སྐུ་གསུང་ཐུགས་དང་ལྡན་པའི་ལྷ་ཉིད་དུ་སྣང་དུ་རུང་མོད་ཀྱི། དེ་ནི་ཀ་བ་ལ་སོགས་པའི་མཚན་ཉིད་མ་ཡིན་ཏེ་ཇི་ལྟར་མི་སྡུག་པ་སྒོམས་པས་ས་ཕྱོགས་རུས་པ་ལ་སོགས་པས་གང་བ་བཞིན་ནོ། །དེ་བཞིན་དུ་ཟད་པར་གྱི་སྐྱེ་མཆེད་ལ་སོགས་པ་སྒོམ་པའི་སྣང་བ་ཡང་དབང་འབྱོར་བའི་གཟུགས་ཏེ། ཆོས་ཀྱི་སྐྱེ་མཆེད་ཀྱི་གཟུགས་ཀྱི་བྱེ་བྲག་ཞིག་ཡིན་པས། དངོས་པོའི་མཚན་ཉིད་མ་ཡིན་ནོ་ཞེས་ཟེར་བ་དང་། ཁ་ཅིག་ན་རེ།[5] ལྷར་སྣང་བའི་ཚེ་རང་གི་སྣང་བ་[6]འགྱུར་བ་[7]ཡིན་པས་མཐུན་པར་སྣང་བའི་མཚན་ཉིད་མ་ཡིན་ནོ། །ཞེས་རྒོལ་བ་ལ། རྣམ་པ་ཡང་ཐ་དད་པ་མ་ཡིན་ཏེ། མཐུན་པར་སྣང་བའི་ཕྱིར་ཞེས་བྱ་བ་བསྟན་པ་ཡིན་ཏེ། ཇི་ལྟར་ཡི་དྭགས་ལ་རྣག་ཏུ་སྣང་བ་ཡང་ལས་མཐུན་རང་གི་སྣང་བ་ཡིན་ལ། ཆུར་སྣང་བ་ཡང་ལས་མཐུན་རང་གི་སྣང་བ་ཡིན་པས་གཞི་ཐ་དད་དོ་ཞེས་བྱ་བར་མི་རུང་སྟེ་གཤེར་བར་མཐུན་པར་སྣང་བ་གཉིས་[8]ག་[9]ལ་མ་ལོག་པས། དེ་བས་ན་གླུང་ཆོས་ཅན་དུ་བྱ་བར་རུང་བ་ཡིན་ཏེ། གལ་ཏེ་དེ་ཡང་དགག་[10]ན། རྣག་ཏུ་[11]སྣང་བ་ཉིད་ཀྱང་རང་རང་གི་སྣང་བ་ཡིན་པས་ཆོས་ཅན་རྒོལ་བ་དང་ཕྱིར་རྒོལ་བ་གཉིས་ག་ལ་གྲུབ་པ་གང་ཡང་རྙེད་པར་མི་འགྱུར་རོ།

1 *RS, C* pa'i
2 *RS* pa'o
3 *CR* ba'i
4 *C* //
5 *CR* om. /
6 *CR* ma 'gyur
7 *CR* pa
8 *RS* gnyi
9 *CR* gal
10 *S* gal te de yang dag go
11 *CR* du

།དེ་བཞིན་དུ་ཐུན་མོང་གི་སྣང་བ་ལ་ལུས་དང་ངག་དང་ཡིད་ཀྱི་རྣམ་པ་མ་དག་པར་སྣང་བ་དང་། ལྷའི་སྐུ་གསུང་ཐུགས་རྡོ་རྗེའི་སྣང་བ་དག་པ་གཉི་[1]ག་ཡང་ལུས་ངག་ཡིད་གསུམ་གྱི་རྣམ་པ་དང་བཅས་པའི་ཞིང་དང་སྤྱོད་ཡུལ་དུ་སྣང་བ་གཉི་ག་ལ་མ་ལོག་པར་མཐུན་པར་སྣང་བས། དེ་བས་ན་འདི་ལྟར་སྣང་བ་ཆོས་ཅན་དུ་བཞག་ཏུ་རུང་བ་ཡིན་ཏེ། གལ་སྟེ་རང་རང་གི་སྣང་བ་ཡིན་པས་ཀུན་ཀྱང་ཐ་དད་དོ་ཞེས་མཐུན་སྣང་བཀག་ན་ཀ་བ་ལ་སོགས་པ་རང་རང་གི་སྣང་བ་ཡིན་པས་ཆོས་ཅན་གྲོལ་བ་དང་ཕྱིར་གྲོལ་བ་གཉི་ག་ལ་གྲུབ་པ་གང་ཡང་རྙེད་པར་མི་འགྱུར་རོ། །དེ་བས་ན་སྣང་བ་ལྟར་བསྒྲུབ་པ་འདི་ཡང་ཆོས་ཅན་ཐ་དད་པའི་ཉེས་པ་མེད་དོ། །ཡང་དྲིས་པ། ཡོངས་སུ་དག་པའི་ལྷ་ནི་ཆོས་ཉིད་དང་ཡེ་ཤེས་ཀྱིས་ཕྱེ་སྟེ་རྣམ་པར་བཞག་པ་མ་ཡིན་ནམ། ཇི་ལྟར་ན་སེམས་ཀྱི་རྣམ་པར་སྣང་བར་འགྱུར་ཞེ་ན། ཡོངས་སུ་དག་པའི་ལྷ་ཡང་རྣམ་པ་གཉིས་ཀྱི་ཚུལ་གྱིས་བཞག་སྟེ། ཇི་ལྟར་མེ་ལོང་གི་གཟུགས་བརྙན་ནི་མེ་ལོང་གི་ཡོན་ཏན་ཡིན་པས། མེ་ལོང་དུ་གཞག་པ་དང་། བྱད་[2]ཀྱི་གཟུགས་བརྙན་ཡིན་པས། བྱད་[3]ཀྱི་རྣམ་པར་བཞག་གོ །དེ་བཞིན་དུ་ལྷའི་སྐུ་གསུང་ཐུགས་སུ་སྣང་བ་ཡང་། ཡེ་ཤེས་ཀྱིས་[4]ཆོས་ཉིད་རྟོགས་པའི་དབང་དང་། ཐུགས་རྗེས་སྨོན་ལམ་བསྒྲུབ་པའི་ཤུགས་ཀྱིས་སྣང་བ་ཡིན་པས། ཡེ་ཤེས་དང་ཆོས་ཉིད་ཀྱིས་ཕྱེ་བའོ། །ཞེས་བཞག་པ་དང་། ལྟར་སྣང་བ་དེ་[5]དག་ཀྱང་བག་ཆགས་དང་བཅས་པའི་སེམས་ཀྱི་རྣམ་པ་སྣང་བ་[6]ཡིན་པས་སེམས་ཉིད་དུ་བསྡུས་པའོ། །དེ་ལ་བག་ཆགས་ཀྱི་རྒྱུས་ཇི་ལྟར་སྣང་ཞེ་ན། དེ་ལ་འཛིན་པ་གཉིས་ཀྱི་བག་ཆགས་ནི། དེ་ཡང་ཡུལ་དང་ཡུལ་ཅན་དུ་སྣང་བར་འགྱུར་རོ། །དཀར་པོ་ལས་

1 *CR* gnyis
2 *C* byang
3 *C* byang
4 *S, CR* kyi
5 *RS* om. de
6 *CR* bas

ཀྱི་བག་ཆགས་ཀྱིས་ནི་མཚན་དང་དཔེ་བྱད་ལ་སོགས་པས་བརྒྱན་པ་ཁྱད་པར་ཅན་དུ་སྣང་བར་འགྱུར། གཞན་ [1] ཡང་བདག་ཏུ་ལྟ་བའི་བག་ཆགས་ཀྱིས་ནི་བདག་དང་ [2] ལྟ་རྒྱུད་སོ་སོར་སྣང་བ་དང་ཡུལ་ཕེག་ [3] ལིང་དུ་ཆད་ [4] པར་སྣང་བར་འགྱུར་རོ། །མངོན་པར་བརྗོད་པའི་བག་ཆགས་ཀྱིས་ནི་མཚན་མ་ [5] ཐ་དད་དུ་སྣང་བར་འགྱུར་རོ། །སྲིད་པ་ཡན་ལག་གི་བག་ཆགས་ལས་ནི་སྐྱེ་བའི་རང་བཞིན་དུ་སྣང་སྟེ། བག་ཆགས་ཐམས་ཅད་མ་ལུས་པར་ཟད་ [6] པ་ལ་ནི་ཡོངས་སུ་དག་པའི་སྤྱོད་ཡུལ་ཡང་སྣང་བ་མ་ཡིན་ནོ། །སངས་རྒྱས་པའི་དག་པ་འཇིག་རྟེན་པའི་ཡེ་ཤེས་ནི། དེ་བཞིན་དུ་ཡོད་དམ་མེད་པ་ནི་བརྟག་པར་བྱ་བ་སྟེ། བསམ་གྱིས་མི་ཁྱབ་པའི་ཆོས་ཡིན་ནོ། །ཡང་དྲིས་པ། ཡོངས་སུ་དག་པའི་ལྷ་ཡུལ་གྱི་བདག་ཉིད་དུ་བཞག་པའི་ཚེ། ཡེ་ཤེས་དང་ཆོས་ཉིད་ཀྱིས་ཕྱེ་བར་བཞག་པ་གང་ཡིན་པ་སྟེ། ཐ་མལ་པའི་སེམས་འཁྲུལ་བར་ [7] སྣང་བའི་བདག་ཉིད་ལ་ཡོད་པ་མ་ཡིན་ནོ་ཞེ་ན། དེ་ཡང་དེ་ལྟར་མ་ཡིན་ཏེ། སོ་སོ་སྐྱེ་བོའི་ཤེས་པའང་རང་བཞིན་གྱིས་རྣམ་པར་བྱང་བའི་མཚན་ཉིད་ཡིན་པ་དང་། ཡེ་ཤེས་ཀྱང་བྱང་ཆུབ་ཀྱི་སེམས་བསྐྱེད་པ་འབའ་ཞིག་ལ་ལྟོས་པ་མ་ཡིན་ཏེ། རང་བྱུང་གི་ཡེ་ཤེས་ཡོད་པར་བདག་ཅག་ལྟ་བུ་གཉིས་ག་ལ་མཐུན་པར་གྲུབ་པའི་མདོ་སྡེ་ལས་གསུངས་ཏེ། འདི་ལྟར་འཕགས་པ་ཤེས་རབ་ཀྱི་ཕ་རོལ་ཏུ་ཕྱིན་པ་ལས། སོ་སོ་སྐྱེ་བའི་ཤེས་པའང་། རང་བཞིན་གྱིས་ནི་རྣམ་བྱང་ཅན། ཞེས་གསུངས་པ་དང་། འཕགས་པ་སྡོང་པོ་བཀོད་པ་ལས། ལྷའི་བུ་རབ་མཆོ་མའི་གནས་སུ་ཆོས་ཀྱི་འཁོར་ལོ་བསྐོར་བའི་ [8] སྐབས་སུ།

1 *CR* instead of gzhan: de
2 *CR* om. dang
3 *CR* beg
4 *RS* ched
5 *CR* om. ma
6 *CR* zang
7 *C* par
8 *CR* pa'i

འཇིག་རྟེན་ཁམས་མང་ལ་ལ་དག །བསམ་གྱིས་མི་ཁྱབ་འཚིག་འགྱུར་ཡང་། །ནམ་མཁའ་འཚིག་པར་མི་འགྱུར་བཞིན། །རང་བྱུང་ཡེ་ཤེས་དེ་བཞིན་ནོ། །ཞེས་གསུངས་ཏེ། གསང་སྔགས་ཀྱི་ཚུལ་ལས་གྲགས་པ་ནི་ལྷག་པར་སྨྲོས་ཀྱང་མི་དགོས་ཏེ། དེ་བས་ན་སྒྲིབ་པ་ཀུན་ནས་རགས་པ་དག་པས་ན་ཐུན་མོང་གི་སྣང་བ་ཕལ་ཆེར་མ་ལོག་ཀྱང་ཞིང་དང་སྤྱོད་ཡུལ་ཡོངས་སུ་དག་པ་སྣང་བར་འགྱུར་རོ། །དེ་བས་ན་ཆོས་ཅན་ཐ་དད་མ་ཡིན་ནོ། །མདོར་བསྡུས་ཏེ་བསྒྲུབ་པར་བྱ་ན་ཇི་སྲིད་དུ་ཡོངས་སུ་དག་པ་དང་མ་དག་པའི་ལུས་དང་སྤྱོད་ཡུལ་དུ་སྣང་བ་ཡུལ་དང་དུས་ལ་སོགས་པ་རྣམ་པས་རབ་ཏུ་ཕྱེ་བ་ཐམས་ཅད་ནི་ཀུན་གཞི་རྣམ་པར་ཤེས་པའི་སྐད་ཅིག་མ་གཅིག་གི་སྣང་བ་ཡིན་པའི་ཕྱིར་གདོད་མ་[1]ཐོབ་[2]པར་བྱ་བའི་ཆོས་ནི་གང་ཡང་མེད་དེ། དཔེར་ན་ནམ་མཁའ་ལ་[3]ནམ་མཁའི་མཚན་ཉིད་སྒྲུབ་ཏུ་མེད་པ་བཞིན་ནོ། །ཞེས་བྱ་བ་འདི་ཡང་སྐྱོན་མེད་པར་གྲུབ་པ་ཡིན་ནོ། །རྣམ་པར་ཤེས་པའི་ཚོགས་བརྒྱད་ཀྱང་ལས་ཀྱིས་ཕྱེ་བར་ཟད་ཀྱི་རིགས་ནི་ཀུན་གཞི་རྣམ་པར་ཤེས་པའི་རིགས་ཉིད་ཡིན་པས་ཐ་དད་པ་མེད་དོ། །བདག་དང་གཞན་གྱི་རྒྱུད་ཀྱང་གང་ཟག་གིས་ཕྱེ་བར་ཟད་ཀྱི་ཆོས་ཀྱིས་ཕྱེ་བ་མ་ཡིན་ནོ། །རིགས་[4]པའང་ཆེ་ཆུང་གི་བྱེ་བྲག་ཡོད་དེ། འཕྲུལ་སྣང་དེ་བཞིན་དུ་ཚད་མར་གྲུབ་པ་ལ་[5]སྣང་བ་ཉིད་ཀྱི་དབང་དུ་སྐྱོན་མེད་པར་ཡང་མ་ཡིན་ནོ། །ཚུལ་དེ་ཉིད་ལ་བློ་དང་ལྡན་པས་བསྒྲུབ་ན། བསྒྲུབ་བྱ་སྒྲུབ་ཏུ་མི་རུང་བ་ཡང་མ་ཡིན་ནོ། །སྣང་བ་ལྷར་བསྒྲུབ་ཆེན་པོ་ཞེས་བྱ་བ་དྷརྨ་[6]བྷ་དྲས་མཛད་པའོ། །དགེའོ།། །།

1 *RS, C* om. ma
2 *RS, C* 'thob
3 *CR* om. la
4 *CR* rig
5 *RS* /
6 *CR* rma'

Bibliography

Sūtra

Saṁdhinirmocanasūtra (*Dgongs pa nges par 'grel pa'i mdo*). 106 in the *Sde dge* edition of the *Bka' 'gyur.*

Indian and Tibetan Authors

Asaṅga. (fourth century) *Abhidharmasamuccaya* (*Chos mngon pa kun las btus pa*). 4049 in the *Sde dge* edition of the *Bstan 'gyur.*

Candrakīrti. (seventh century) *Madhyamakāvatāra* (*Dbu ma la 'jug pa*). 3861 in the *Sde dge* edition of the *Bstan 'gyur.*

Do-ngag Tenpay Nyima (Mdo sngags bstan pa'i nyi ma). (d. 1959) *Differentiation of Views and Tenets* (*Lta grub shan 'byed gnad kyi sgron me'i rtsa 'grel*). Chengdu: Si khron mi rigs dpe skrun khang, 1996.

Gö Khugpa Lhetse ('Gos khug pa lhas btsas). (eleventh century) *Discourse on Guhyasamāja* (*Gsang 'dus stong thun*). New Delhi: Trayang, 1973.

Gö Lotsāwa ('Gos lo tsā ba). (1392-1481) *Blue Annals* (*Deb ther sngon po*). Varanasi: Vajra Vidya Institute, 2003.

Jamgon Kongtrul ('Jam mgon kong sprul). (1813-1899) *The Lapis Lazuli Garland* (*Zab mo'i gter dang gter ston grub thob ji ltar byon pa'i lo rgyus mdor bsdus bkod pa rin chen vaiḍūrya'i phreng ba*). In *Rin chen gter mdzod*, vol. 1, pp. 291-759. Paro, Bhutan: Lama Ngodrup and Sherab Drimey, 1976.

_______. *Treasury of Knowledge* (*Shes bya kun khyab mdzod*). 3 vols. Beijing: Mi rigs dpe skrun khang, 1982.

Karma Phuntsho. *Steps to Valid Cognition* (*Tshad ma'i stan bcos rigs pa'i them skas*). Bylakuppe: Ngagyur Nyingma Institute, 1997.

Kunzang Palden (Kun bzang dpal ldan). (nineteenth century) *Commentary to the Beacon of Certainty* (*Nges shes sgron me rtsa 'grel*). Chengdu: Si khron mi rigs dpe skrun khang, 1997.

Lochen Dharma Śrī (Lo chen dharma śrī). (1654-1718) *Speech of the Lord of Secrets* (*Rtsa rgyud sgyu 'phrul gsang ba snying po'i spyi don gsang bdag zhal lung*), vol. 8. Delhi: Jayyed Press, 1977.

Longchen Rabjam (Klong chen rab byams). (1308-1363) *Relaxing into the Natural State of Mind* (*Rdzogs pa chen po sems nyid ngal gso'i 'grel pa shing rta chen po*). Odiyan: Dharmacakra Press, 1994.

———. *Treasury of Philosophical Tenets* (*Grub pa'i mtha' rin po che'i mdzod*). Odiyan: Dharmacakra Press, 1991.

———. *Wish-fulfilling Treasury* (*Yid bzhin rin po che'i mdzod*). Odiyan: Dharmacakra Press, 1991.

Mipham (Mi pham rgya mtsho). (1846-1912) *Beacon of Certainty* (*Nges shes rin po che'i sgron me*). In Kunzang Palden, *Commentary to the Beacon of Certainty* (*Nges shes sgron me rtsa 'grel*). Chengdu: Si khron mi rigs dpe skrun khang, 1997.

———. *Gateway to Knowledge* (*Mkhas pa'i tshul la 'jug pa'i mgo*). Xining: Mtsho sngon mi rigs dpe skrun khang, 1994.

———. *Ketaka Jewel* (*Shes rab kyi le'u 'grel pa nor bu ke ta ka*). In *Sde-Dge Dgon-Chen Prints of the Writings of 'Jam-Mgon 'Ju Mi-Pham-Rgya-Mtsho*, vol. 14, pp. 1-96. Kathmandu: Shechen Monastery, c. 1990.

———. *Speech of Delight* (*Dbu ma rgyan gyi rnam bshad 'jam dbyangs bla ma dgyes pa'i zhal lung*). In Ju Mipham, *Speech of Delight: Mipham's Commentary on Śāntarakṣita's* Ornament of the Middle Way. Ithaca: Snow Lion Publications, 2004.

———. *Survey of the Guhyagarbha* (*Gsang rnying spyi don 'od gsal snying po*). Chengdu: Si khron mi rigs dpe skrun khang, 2000.

———. *Sword of Wisdom*. In Palden Sherab, *Commentary to the Sword of Wisdom* (*Don rnam par nges pa shes rab ral gri'i 'grel pa shes rab nyi zla 'bar ba'i sgron me*). Varanasi, Satnam Printing Press, 2000.

Padmasambhava. (eighth century) *Garland of Views as Oral Instructions* (*Man ngag lta ba'i phreng ba*). In *Rongzom chos bzang gi gsung 'bum*, vol. 1, pp. 291-300. Chengdu: Si khron mi rigs dpe skrun khang, 1999.

Palden Sherab (Dpal ldan shes rab). (b. 1941) *Commentary to the Sword of Wisdom* (*Don rnam par nges pa shes rab ral gri'i 'grel pa shes rab nyi zla 'bar ba'i sgron me*). Varanasi, Satnam Printing Press, 2000.

Rongzom (Rong zom chos kyi bzang po). (eleventh century) *Black Snake Discourse* (*Sbrul nag po'i stong thun*). In *Rongzom chos bzang gi gsung 'bum*, vol. 2, pp. 66-69. Chengdu: Si khron mi rigs dpe skrun khang, 1999.

———. *Commentary to the Guhyagarbha Tantra* (*Rgyud rgyal gsang ba snying po dkon mchog 'grel*). In *Rongzom chos bzang gi gsung 'bum*, vol. 1, pp. 33-250. Chengdu: Si khron mi rigs dpe skrun khang, 1999.

_______. *Commentary to the Weapon of Speech* (*Sma sgo mtshon cha'i 'grel ba*). In *Rongzom chos bzang gi gsung 'bum*, vol. 2, pp. 415-455. Chengdu: Si khron mi rigs dpe skrun khang, 1999.

_______. *Entering the Way of the Great Vehicle* (*Theg pa chen po'i tshul la 'jug pa*). In *Rongzom chos bzang gi gsung 'bum*, vol. 2, pp. 417-555. Chengdu: Si khron mi rigs dpe skrun khang, 1999.

_______. *Establishing Appearances as Divine* (*Snang ba lhar bsgrub*). In *Rongzom chos bzang gi gsung 'bum*, vol. 2, pp. 559-568. Chengdu: Si khron mi rigs dpe skrun khang, 1999.

_______. *Memorandum on Views* (*Lta ba'i brjed byang chen mo*). In *Rongzom chos bzang gi gsung 'bum*, vol. 2, pp. 1-26 Chengdu: Si khron mi rigs dpe skrun khang, 1999.

Sakya Paṇḍita (Sa skya paṇḍita). (1182-1251) In Sakya Pandita, *A Clear Differentiation of the Three Codes: Essential Distinctions among the Individual Liberation, Great Vehicle, and Tantric Systems.* Trans. Jared Rhoton. Albany: SUNY Press, 2002.

Trisong Deutsen (Khri srong lde'u btsan). (eighth century) *Valid Means of Cognition* (*Bka' yang dag pa'i tshad ma las mdo btus*). 4352 in the *Sde dge* edition of the *Bstan 'gyur*.

Tsongkhapa (Tsong kha pa). (1357-1419) *Stages of Mantra* (*Rgyal ba khyab bdag rdo rje 'chang chen po'i lam gyi rim pa gsang ba kun gyi gnad rnam par phye ba*). Xining: Mtsho sngon mi rigs dpe skrun khang, 1995.

Yungton Dorje Pal (G.yung ston rdo rje dpal). (1284-1365) *Mirror Illuminating the Guhyagarbha Tantra* (*Gsang snying rgyud don gsal byed me long*). In Sanje Dorje, ed., *Commentaries on the Guhyagarbha Tantra and Other Rare Nyingmapa Texts from the Library of Dudjom Rinpoche* (*Bka' ma rgyas pa*), vol. 28. Kalimpong, India: Dupjung Lama, 1982-1987.

Modern Research and Translations

Almogi, Orna. (2002) "Sources on the Life and Works of the Eleventh-Century Tibetan Scholar Rong zom Chos kyi Bzang po: A Brief Survey." In H. Blezer, ed., *Tibet, Past and Present.* Leiden: Brill, 67-80.

Dalton, Jacob. (2005) " A Crisis in Doxography: How Tibetans Organized Tantra During the 8th-12th Centuries." *Journal of the International Association of Buddhist Studies* 28: 115-181.

Davidson, Ronald. (2002) "Gsar ma Apocrypha: the Creation of Orthodoxy, Gray Texts, and the New Revelation." In H. Eimer and D. Germano, eds., *The Many Canons of Tibetan Buddhism.* Leiden: Brill, 203-224.

Doctor, Andreas. (2005) *Tibetan Treasure Literature: Revelation, Tradition, and Accomplishment in Visionary Buddhism.* Ithaca: Snow Lion Publications.

Dreyfus, Georges. (2003) "Would the True Prāsaṅgika Please Stand? The Case and View of 'Ju Mipham." In Dreyfus and McClintock (2003), 317-347.

Dreyfus, Georges, and Sara McClintock, eds. (2003) *The Svātantrika-Prāsaṅgika Distinction: What Difference Does a Difference Make?* Boston: Wisdom Publications.

Dudjom, Rinpoche. (1991) *The Nyingma School of Tibetan Buddhism: Its Fundamentals and History.* 2 vols. G. Dorje and M. Kapstein, trans. and eds. Boston: Wisdom Publications.

Eastman, Kenneth W. (1983). "Mahāyoga Texts at Tun-huang." *Bulletin of Institute of Buddhist Cultural Studies, Ryukoku University* 22: 42-60.

Germano, David. (1992) "Poetic Thought, the Intelligent Universe, and the Mystery of Self: The Tantric Synthesis of Rdzogs Chen in Fourteenth Century Tibet." Ph.D. dissertation, University of Wisconsin.

_______. (1994) "Architecture and Absence in the Secret Tantric History of the Great Perfection." *Journal of the International Association of Buddhist Studies* 17: 203-335.

Gyatso, Janet. (1995) "Drawn from the Tibetan Treasury: The *gTer ma* Literature." In J.Cabezón and R. Jackson, eds., *Tibetan Literature: Studies in Genre.* Ithaca: Snow Lion Publications, 147-169.

Hayes, Richard P. (1994). "Nāgārjuna's Appeal." *Journal of Indian Philosophy* 22: 299-378.

Jackson, David. (1994). *Enlightenment by a Single Means.* Wien: Verlag der Österreichischen Akademie der Wissenschaften.

Kajiyama, Yuichi. (1973) "Three kinds of affirmation and two kinds of negation in Buddhist philosophy." *Wiener Zeitschrift zur Kunde Südasiens* 17: 161-175.

Kapstein, Matthew. (1996) "gDams ngag: Tibetan Technologies of the Self." In J. Cabezón and R. Jackson, eds., *Tibetan Literature: Studies in Genre*. Ithaca: Snow Lion Publications, 275-289.

_______. (2000) *The Tibetan Assimilation of Buddhism: Conversion, Contestation, and Memory.* Oxford: Oxford University Press.

_______. (2002) *Reason's Traces: Identity and Interpretation in Indian and Tibetan Buddhist Thought*. Boston: Wisdom Publications.

Karmay, Samten. (1988) *The Great Perfection (rDzogs Chen): A Philosophical and Meditative Tradition in Tibetan Buddhism*. Leiden: Brill.

Komarovski, Iaroslav. (2000) *Three Texts on Madhyamaka by Shakya Chokden*. Dharamsala: Library of Tibetan Works and Archives.

Lang, Karen. (1990) "Spa-tshab Nyi-ma-grags and the Introduction of Prāsaṅgika Madhyamaka into Tibet." In L. Epstein and R. Sherburne, eds., *Reflections on Tibetan Culture: Essays in Memory of Turrell V. Wylie.* Studies in Asian Thought and Religion 12. Lewiston/ Queenston/ Lampeter: The Edwin Mellen Press, 127-141.

Lessing, F.D., and A. Wayman. (1983) *Introduction to the Buddhist Tantric Systems*. Delhi: Motilal Banarsidass.

Lipman, Kennard. (1992) "What Is Buddhist Logic? Some Tibetan Developments of Pramāṇa Theory." In S. Goodman and R. Davidson, eds., *Tibetan Buddhism: Reason and Revelation*. Albany: SUNY Press, 25-44.

Lopez, Donald. (2000) "A Tantric Meditation on Emptiness." In D. White, ed., *Tantra in Practice*. Princeton: Princeton University Press, 523-542.

Mimaki, Katsumi. (1994) "Doxographie tibétaine et classifications indiennes." In F. Fumimasa and G. Fussman, eds., *Bouddhisme et cultures locales: quelques cas de réciproques adaptations*. Actes du colloque franco-japonais de septembre 1991. Paris: École française d'Extrême-Orient, 115-136.

Mipham, Ju. (2003) *Speech of Delight: Mipham's Commentary on Śāntrakṣita's Ornament of the Middle Way*. Trans. T. Doctor. Ithaca: Snow Lion Publications.

Nagao, Gadjin. (1994) *An Index to Asaṅga's Mahāyānasaṁgraha*. Studia Philologica Buddhica, Monograph Series 9. Tokyo: The International Institute for Buddhist Studies.

Napper, Elizabeth. (1989) *Dependent Arising and Emptiness*. Boston: Wisdom Publications.

Obermiller, E. (1996) *The History of Buddhism in India and Tibet by Bu Ston*. New Delhi: Paljor Publications.

Pettit, John. (1999) *Beacon of Certainty: Illuminating the View of Dzogchen, the Great Perfection*. Boston: Wisdom Publications.

Roerich, George. (1979) *Blue Annals*. Delhi: Motilal Banarsidass.

Ruegg, David Seyfort. (1981) *The Literature of the Madhyamaka School of Philosophy in India*. A History of Indian Literature, vol. 7, fasc. 1. Wiesbaden: Otto Harrassowitz.

Sakya Pandita. (2002) *A Clear Differentiation of the Three Codes: Essential Distinctions among the Individual Liberation, Great Vehicle, and Tantric Systems*. Trans. Jared Rhoton. Albany: SUNY Press.

Snellgrove, David. (1987) *Indo-Tibetan Buddhism: Indian Buddhists and Their Tibetan Successors*. Boston: Shambhala.

Tauscher, Helmut. (1995). *Die Lehre von den zwei Wircklichkeiten in Tsong kha pas Madhyamaka-Werken*. Vienna: Arbeitskreis für Tibetische und Buddistische Studien.

_______. (2003) "Phya pa chos kyi seng ge as a Svātantrika." In Dreyfus and McClintock (2003), 207-255.

Tillemans, Tom. (2003) "Metaphysics for Mādhyamikas." In Dreyfus and McClintock (2003), 93-123.

Tsuda, Shinichi. (1965) "Classification of Tantras in dPal brtsegs's lTa ba'i rim pa bshad pa and Its Problems." *Journal of Indian and Buddhist Studies*, 13 (1): 402-397.

Tucci, Giuseppe. (1988) *Rin-chen-bzang-po and the Renaissance of Buddhism in Tibet Around the Millenium*. Indo-Tibetica 2. Delhi: Aditya Prakashan.

van Schaik, Sam. (2002) "The Role of Atiyoga in Early Tibetan Tantric Practice." In *The XIII International Association of Buddhist Studies Conference: Abstracts.* Bangkok: Chulalongkorn University.

Vitali, Roberto. (1996) *The Kingdoms of Gu.ge Pu.hrang: According to mNga'.ris rgyal.rabs by Gu.ge mkhan.chen Ngag.dbang grags.pa*. Dharamsala: Tho.ling gtsug.lag.khang lo.gcig.stong 'khor.ba'i rjes.dran.mdzad sgo'i go.sgrig tshogs. chung.

Wangchuk, Dorji. (2002) "An Eleventh-Century Defence of the Authenticity of the Guhyagarbha Tantra." In H. Eimer and D. Germano, eds., *The Many Canons of Tibetan Buddhism*. Leiden: Brill, 265-291.

Yoshimizu, Chizuko. (1996) "Saṃdhinirmocanasūtra X ni okeru shishu no yukti ni tsuite (On the Four Kinds of yukti in the Tenth Chapter of the Saṃdhinirmocanasūtra)." *Journal of Naritasan Institute for Buddhist Studies* 19: 123-168.

Notes

1 For the benefit of the reader not familiar with the Tibetan and Sanskrit languages, I have throughout this book translated technical terms into English while providing the transliterated Tibetan and Sanskrit in parentheses. When referring to Tibetan texts, I supply concise English translations of their titles. Transliteration of the Tibetan titles according to the Wylie system is provided in the footnotes on their first occurrence. The Indian texts I refer to are all classics of Buddhism and I have therefore not translated their titles but kept them in Sanskrit for the sake of general recognition. As for Tibetan personal and place names, I have rendered these in a way that should make them pronounceable to readers not familiar with the quite complex rules of Tibetan spelling and transliteration. Wylie transliteration of these names is provided on their first occurrence.

2 Rong zom chos kyi bzang po. Hereinafter, Rongzom.

3 Although we may retrospectively call Rongzom a Nyingma proponent, the term Nyingma was not yet commonly used during the eleventh century. The expression "early translations" (*snga 'gyur*) may have referred to a distinct spiritual tradition.

4 In researching Rongzom's life and spiritual environment I have relied on a number of secondary sources for the study of the eleventh century, for instance, Roerich (1979), Tucci (1988), Obermiller (1996), Dudjom (1991), and Vitali (1996). Karmay's study on the Great Perfection (Karmay: 1988) and Almogi's survey of Rongzom's biographies and literary corpus (Almogi: 2002) proved especially helpful.

5 Klong chen rab 'jam. Primary sources include the *Precious Wish-fulfilling Treasury* (*Yid bzhin mdzod*), *Precious Treasury of Philosophical Tenets* (*Grub mtha' mdzod*), and *Relaxing into the Natural State of Mind* (*Sems nyid ngal gso*).

6 Lochen's (Lo chen dharma śrī) *Speech of the Lord of Secrets* (*Rtsa rgyud sgyu 'phrul gsang ba snying po'i spyi don gsang bdag zhal lung*) is, for instance, a gold mine for further research with regard to the importation of sūtric terms at the esoteric level.

7 Mipham's ('Ju mi pham) "Survey" (*Spyi don*) of the *Guhyagarbha Tantra* presents a succinct treatment of the issue of the superior view and logical arguments at the esoteric level.

8 Mdo sngags bstan pa'i nyi ma.

9 *Collected Works of Rongzom,* vol. 1, 291-300.

10 Rongzom's initial thesis in *Establishing Appearances as Divine* ([*Collected Works of Rongzom*, vol. 1, 559]: *gsang snags rdo rje theg pa'i tshul las 'jig rten dang 'jig rten las*

'das pa'i chos thams cad dbyer med par sku gsung thugs rdo rje lta bu'i dkyil 'khor du/ ye nas sangs rgyas pa yin pas da lam gyis sgrub pa lta bu ni ma yin no/ "The Vajra vehicle of Secret Mantra states, 'All mundane and supramundane phenomena, without any distinction, are primordially enlightened as the maṇḍala of vajralike body, speech and mind. Thus [the maṇḍala] is not accomplished through a path.'") is strikingly similar to Padmasambhava's *Garland of Views as Oral Instructions* (*Collected Works of Rongzom,* vol. 1, 295) in which the way of Dzogchen (Rdzogs chen) is defined: *rdzogs pa chen po'i tshul ni/ 'jig rten dang 'jig rten las 'das pa'i chos thams cad dbyer med par sku gsung thugs kyi dkyil 'khor gyi rang bzhin ye nas yin par rtogs nas sgom pa ste/* Later in the same text (297) Padmasambhava continues to explain: *de yang chos thams cad ye nas sang rgyas pa'i rang bzhin du lam gyis bsgrub cing nyen pos bcos su med par rtogs pa'o/ . . . de yang chos thams cad ye nas sang rgyas pa'i rang bzhin yin pas/ bdag nyid kyang ye nas lha rang bzhin yin gyi da lta sgrub pa ni ma yin par rtogs pa'o/*

11 See Karmay (1988): 138.

12 On the doxographical dimensions of Mahāyoga, see chapter 2.1.

13 Germano (1994).

14 According to Tibetan historians, during the early dissemination at the historical Samye (Bsam yas) debate it was determined which brand of Buddhism—the Chinese suddenist (*cig car ba*) approach or the gradualist (*rim gyis pa*) approach propagated by Śāntarakṣita and Kamalaśīla—was to be followed. This controversy did not end with the Samye debate, for over the next centuries teachings emphasizing a suddenist approach, such as Dzogchen and Mahāmudrā, found themselves under attack from other traditions, which compared them to the "mindless teachings" of the Chinese master Mo Ho Yen. For more information see D. Jackson (1994). Although the terms "gradualist" and "suddenist" are associated with the debate between Kamalaśīla and the Chinese master Mo Ho Yen, they are nevertheless often used in Tibetan Buddhist discourse without any such connotations. While the question of whether the suddenist trend in the approach of Rongzom and other Nyingma masters was influenced by the Chinese Ch'an school surely is relevant, one must be cautious about inferring such influences. The tension between gradual and more sudden approaches to realization is perhaps intrinsic to much of Buddhist soteriology and thus its mere surfacing cannot in itself be taken as an indication of Chinese influence.

15 *Establishing Appearances as Divine* reflects a number of tensions within the spiritual environment of the eleventh century, such as that between gradualist and suddenist approaches. Rongzom underscores the direct and affirmative Nyingma approach to the issue of purity by introducing mahāyānic tools of reasoning on the esoteric level. Thus he attempts to make the Nyingma suddenist approach more acceptable to an audience that otherwise leaned towards gradualism and sought to ground the esoteric teachings firmly on the basis of the exoteric. As is often the case in Buddhist treatises, Rongzom makes use of an imaginary opponent (*pūrvapakṣa*) to highlight his agenda of validating purity as a sound principle. This opponent appears as a follower of the Mahāyāna teachings inclined to an approach of gradual purification who can only accept the natural and immediate purity of all appearances if presented with an array of dialectical means.

16 See for instance the first page of Yungton Dorje's (G.yung ston rdo rje) commentary

on chapter 13 of the *Guhyagarbha Tantra*. *Bka' ma rgyas pa,* vol. 28, 430.3-4. (Thanks to James Gentry for this reference.)

17 Just as one would, for example, need to examine Tsongkhapa's Svātantrika to be able to appreciate his Prāsaṅgika.

18 Many of Rongzom's central Madhyamaka treatments appear to have been lost and any conclusions in this area must therefore be tentative.

19 *Nges shes sgron me'i rtsa 'grel.*

20 *Dbu ma rgyan gyi rnam bshad 'jam dbyangs bla ma dgyes pa'i zhal lung.* In terms of secondary sources, Pettit's Mipham study (Pettit: 1999) proved a valuable reference.

21 *Bka' yang dag pa'i tshad ma las mdo btus.*

22 Khri srong lde'u btsan.

23 As for secondary sources, Kapstein's treatment of Mipham's four principles (Kapstein: 2002) was illuminating here, as was Yoshimizu's study of the principles in Indian sources (Yoshimizu: 1996).

24 Based on works such as Mipham's *Survey of the Guhyagarbha Tantra* and Do-ngag Tenpay Nyima's *Differentiation of Views and Tenets* (*Lta grub shan 'byed gnad kyi sgron me*), and with recourse to Lipman (1992) and Pettit (1999).

25 See Kapstein (1996) for a fine description of these developments. Atīśa's main disciple, the layman Drom Tonpa ('Brom ston) (1104-1163) founded the Kadampa (Bka' dam pa) school, which was to exercise a deep influence on religion in Tibet up to the present and thus long after its own disappearance as a distinct tradition in the fifteenth century. The practices of Shijey (*zhi byed*) and Choyul (*gcod yul*) are said to have originated from the Indian yogin Phadampa Sangye (Pha dam pa sangs rgyas) and his Tibetan disciple Machig Labdron (Ma cig lab sgron) (ca.1055-1143). The translator Marpa (Mar pa) (1012-1097) is known as the founder of the Kagyu (Bka' brgyud) lineage and as the Tibetan successor to the practices known as the Six Doctrines of Nāropa (Na ro chos drug). The teachings of the Shangpa Kagyu (Shang pa Bka' brgyud), originating from the Indian yoginī Niguma, were introduced by Kyungpo Naljor Tshultrim Gonpo (Khyung po rnal 'byor Tshul khrims mgon po) of Shang (Shangs) (d. ca. 1135). Drogmi Lotsāwa ('Brog mi lo tsā ba) (992-1072) introduced the teachings of Lamdrey (Lam 'bras), which were to become the central teachings of the Sakya (Sa skya) school. Germano comments on this period: "The eleventh to twelfth century witnessed the flowering (and in many cases simultaneous withering) of a tremendous variety of yogic systems experientially based upon the human body and claiming to offer comprehensive systems to arrive at the ultimate realization of Buddhahood." (Germano (1994): 303)

26 Pho phrang shi ba' i 'od.

27 Lha bla ma ye she 'od.

28 See Pettit (1999): 88.

29 On terma (*gter ma*), see Gyatso (1995) and Doctor (2005).

30 Germano (1994): 269.

31 'Jam mgon kong sprul.

32 Jamgon Kongtrul offers a brief description of Rongzom's treasures in his hagiographical survey of the treasure revealers (*gter ston*). Interestingly, although Kongtrul notes that Rongzom's original treasures no longer are extant, he states that a visionary tradition of Rongzom's revelations was revived by Jamyang Khyentse Wangpo ('Jam

dbyangs mkhyen brtse'i dbang po) (1820-1892). See Jamgon Kongtrul, *Lapis Lazuli Garland* (1976): 484.2-4.

33 Yol bge bsnyen rdo rje dbang phyug.

34 Gyag rdo rje 'dzin pa chen po. For more information on Rongzom's biographies, see Almogi (2002).

35 Atīśa—one of the central figures in the Later Dissemination—is reported to have arrived in the Guge (Gu ge) kingdom in 1042. Gö Lotsāwa ('Gos lo tsā ba) (1392-1481) appears to be the first scholar to discuss Rongzom's dates in the *Blue Annals* (*Deb ther sngon po*). See Almogi (2002): 70.

36 See Almogi (2002): 67.

37 See Almogi (2002): 75.

38 *Rje dharma bha dras mdzad pa'i chos kyi rnam grangs kyi tho yig.* See Almogi (2002).

39 Rong pa me dpung.

40 Almogi (2002): 76.

41 See Wangchuk (2002): 269.

42 Karmay mentions that, "The *Theg chen tshul 'jug* may be considered the most important treatise on Rdzogs chen written in the eleventh century that has come to light." (Karmay (1988): 126)

43 Rongpa Mepung's index (*tho yig*) often lists three versions of the same text in triads of "greater, intermediate, and lesser" (*chen po, 'bring ba, chung ba*) versions.

44 *Snang ba lhar sgrub che phra bdun du grags pa* (*Collected Works of Rongzom,* vol. 2, 239).

45 It may have been Jigme Lingpa ('Jig med gling pa) who first attempted to connect Rongzom with Longchen Rabjam, a project which was then intensified by Mipham. See Almogi (2002): 73.

46 Jamgon Kongtrul (1976): 484.2 hails Rongzom as a reincarnation of the famed translator Vairocana.

47 'Gos khug pa lhas btsas.

48 *Deb ther sngon po*, vol. 1, 209.

49 Ibid., 209.

50 On the question of authenticity as an issue of geography or ethnicity, see Davidson (2002): 203.

51 His commentary on the *Guhyagarbha Tantra* is an important exception.

52 For example, Rongzom's opponent and contemporary, Gö Khugpa Lhetse, begins his treatise (*Gsang 'dus stong thun*) on the *Guhyasamāja* practice with the traditional homage and the *Valid Means of Cognition* attributed to Trisong Deutsen also features an elaborate homage. Likewise, the *Garland of Views as Oral Instructions* attributed to Padmasambhava features an initial homage while Rongzom's commentary on this text does not.

53 *Collected Works of Rongzom,* vol. 1, 417: *theg pa chen po'i tshul la 'jug pa mdo tsam brjod pa/*

54 *Collected Works of Rongzom,* vol. 2, 415: *bar gcod spang bar bya ba dang/ ya rabs kyi tshul dang thun par bya ba'i phyir/ dang por phyag 'tshal nas/*

55 On the other hand, given that Tibetan compositions were generally controversial during that time, all such compositions might, to a certain extent, have been viewed

as "private production." Perhaps it would have seemed inappropriately bold to use stylistic features of the Indian śāstras, such as a traditional homage or a denial of "private production," in a Tibetan composition. Thus Rongzom's omissions could also be interpreted as a conservative yielding to the social pressures of the time.

56 See Davidson (2002): 211-212.

57 See Kapstein (2000): 89. Although the dialectical approach of the Madhyamaka and the logic and epistemology of Buddhist *pramāṇa* had been introduced to Tibet during the eighth century, a renewed interest in these subjects is evident from the middle of the eleventh century.

58 Another striking feature of Rongzom's writings is the abundance of analogies and anecdotes. Although some of these are drawn from Sūtra literature, they lend a further element of lively creativity to his discourse.

59 When treating the views of thinkers from several time periods as members of a uniform "Nyingma tradition," one runs the risk of simplifying, if not erasing, distinctions that are important for an understanding of the history of ideas. However, when aligning the views of individual masters who claim allegiance to the same tradition, certain common traits may emerge that provide significant insights into the nature of the philosophical themes that these authors discuss. Determining such traits may be relevant for appraising and contextualizing Rongzom's view on Mantra and Sūtra and for his project of establishing appearances as pure.

60 Dalton claims that the Sanskrit reconstruction "*Anuttarayogatantra" for the Tibetan term *rnal 'byor bla med* is a mistake, and that available Sanskrit manuscripts instead suggest that *rnal 'byor bla med* more often translates "Yoganiruttara." See Dalton (2005): 152, n. 84. In the Tibetan tradition *rnal 'byor bla med* is further subdivided by the proponents of the New Schools into a dyadic or triadic internal division.

61 See Germano (1994): 247, n. 114.

62 There has been debate about whether the three higher tantras (Mahā, Anu, and Ati) were set forth as individual vehicles in the early stages of Buddhism in Tibet. However, Sam van Schaik has found clear indications in Tunhuang documents that the term "nine gradual vehicles" (*theg pa rim pa dgu*) was in use very early (see van Schaik (2002): 235-236). Also, the *Garland of Views as Oral Instructions* explains the different approaches to enlightenment by means of nine categories, of which the first six have the name "vehicle" (*theg pa, yāna*) attached, while the last three are merely called "ways" (*tshul*). Rongzom in his *Commentary on the Guhyagarbha Tantra* clearly identifies these nine categories explained in the *Garland of Views as Oral Instructions* as nine vehicles (*theg pa dgu*): *theg pa ni rnam pa dgur bstan pa yang yod de/ man ngag lta ba'i phreng ba las gsungs pa ltar/ mtshan nyid sde gsum dang/ phyi rgyud sde gsum dang/ nang rgyud sde gsum mo/* (*Collected Works of Rongzom*, vol. 1, 47). Karmay, when discussing Sapaṇ's criticism of the nine vehicles (*theg pa dgu*), states that, "His [Sa paṇ's] contention is not simply philosophical pedantry as it might seem. It has the echo of a distant tradition in the past where *Atiyoga* was not considered to be a *theg pa*." Karmay supports this with explanations found in Tunhuang documents as well as in the *Garland of Views as Oral Instructions* and Rongzom's *Commentary to the Garland of Views as Oral Instructions*, where the authors (including Rongzom) have refrained from using the term "vehicle" (*theg pa*) for the

last three of the nine vehicles (*theg pa dgu*) (Karmay (1988): 148). However, we must with reference to the above cited passage from his commentary to the *Guhyagarbha Tantra* note that Rongzom had no reservation with regard to classifying each of the six classes of Tantra, set forth in the *Garland of Views as Oral Instructions*, as a distinct vehicle (*theg pa*).

63 Sapaṇ may have been the first critic of the nine-vehicle (*theg pa dgu*) system, calling *Yoga, Mahāyoga, Anuyoga,* and *Atiyoga* mere levels of meditative absorptions (*samādhi*) and objecting to them being termed *yānas*. He particularly objects to the classification of *Atiyoga* as a vehicle (*theg pa*) since it is wisdom (*ye shes*) (see Karmay (1988): 147 and Sakya Pandita (2002): 132-133). When explaining the connotations of the term "vehicle" (*theg pa*) in the context of the *Guhyagarbha,* Rongzom remarks that "vehicle" (*theg pa*) here refers both to the mind that realizes equality and to the scriptures that teach it: *'dir ni mnyam pa nyid rtogs pa'i blo dang/ de ston pa'i gzhung gi tshig gnyis ka la theg pa'i sgrar bshad do//* (*Collected Works of Rongzom,* vol. 1, 46). Dudjom addresses Sapaṇ's critique, referring to Sapaṇ's assertion that "Atiyoga is not a vehicle," as a statement that requires interpretation (*dgongs pa can*) (see Dudjom (1991): 907-908). Mipham's *Survey of the Guhyagarbha Tantra* takes up Sapaṇ's critique in detail (see Mipham: 2000).

64 The following definition of this term is found in *Relaxing into the Natural State of Mind* (485b-486a): *de dag gi rim pa so sor bshad pa/ de yang bya spyod rnal 'byor thub pa rgyud/kri ya u pa yo ga zhes bya'o/de yang kri ya ste bya ba dang/u pa ya ste spyod pa dang/yo ga ste rnal 'byor dang/tandra ste rgyud du grags pa de gsum ni thub pas gsungs pa phyi mtshan nyid kyi theg pa ltar gtsang sbra dang sdom pa'i kun spyod kyi tshul mdzungs pas thub pa rgyud kyi theg pa zhes bya'o/* "If one were to explain these stages one by one, then action, conduct, and union, [i.e.,] the Sage tantras, are called respectively *Kriyā, Upa,* and *Yoga. Kriyā* means 'action,' while *Upaya* refers to 'conduct' and *Yoga* to 'union.' These are *tantras,* i.e., [what in Tibetan is translated as] 'continuum' [rgyud]. Since regarding the conduct these three resemble discipline and cleanliness [observed in] the outer *yāna* of dialectics taught by the Sage, they are known as the 'Tantrayāna of the Sage.'" Note that the term *thub pa rgyud kyi theg pa* here is explained with reference to the Buddha, "the Sage." However, in most other texts, the word *thub pa* tends to be understood in terms of capacity, as evinced for example in *Collected Works of Rongzom,* vol. 1, 332-333.

65 The Ubhayā tantra is of particular interest, since this classification appears at times interchangeable with the term "Caryā." Longchen Rabjam, for instance, in *Relaxing into the Natural State of Mind,* first uses the term "Upaya" (Ubhayā) in accordance with the classification of earlier Nyingma scholars such as Rongzom, but then proceeds to explain this to be "conduct" (*spyod pa*), thus aligning his exegesis with the classification model of the New Tantras (*sngags gsar ma*).

Mimaki has made a similar observation: "Dans le *Grub mtha' mdzod* de Klong chen rab 'byams pa, ce véhicule est appelé ubhayātantra comme il l'est ordinairement, mais dans son *Yid bzhin mdzod* il est dit que l'ubhayātantra est aussi appelé caryātantra. Doit-on voir lá un effort pour rapprocher la classification des Nyingma pa de celle des Gsar ma pa?" (Mimaki (1994): 125-126)

While it seems that for some later Nyingma scholars, such as Longchen Rabjam, Caryā and Ubhayā appeared to be mere synonyms, it is likely that Ubhayā and Caryā were earlier used as distinct classifications of Tantra (see Tsuda (1965): 398-399).

66 Kongtrul in his *Treasury of Knowledge* (*Shes bya kun khyab*) (vol. 1, 735) remarks when treating the Nyingma school that the explanation of the six classifications (Śrāvaka, Pratyekabuddha, Bodhisattva, Caryā, Ubhayā, Yoga) does not differ from the new tantras to the extent that they need separate explanations.

67 For instance, Lochen explains the Kriyā view of the relative as follows (*Speech of the Lord of Secrets*, 31a): *kun rdzob la/ yang log gnyis las/ log pa'i kun rdzob ni/ dbu ma pa man chad kyis yang dag dang log par rtags pa'i kun rdzob thams cad yin la/ yang dag kun rdzob ni/ chos nyid rtogs pa'i yon tan rigs gsum lha'i dkyil 'khor du snang bar 'dod pa ste/* "As for the relative truth there are two [principles]: the mistaken relative includes all that by the Mādhyamikas and below is thought of as the mistaken and the authentic relative. The authentic relative is considered to be the qualities of realizing the intrinsic nature appearing as the maṇḍala of the three types of divinities."

It is interesting to note that, even according to the lower levels of Tantra, all the properties of an authentic and a mistaken relative truth, as set forth in the Madhyamaka and other dialectical schools, are thrown together into one pot: the mistaken relative truth. Hence, at any level of Mantra, anything conceived of as impure is necessarily, according to Lochen, a mistaken perception for the Nyingma adept. In the context of defining the view of the Yogatantra, Lochen reiterates (*Speech of the Lord of Secrets*, 33a): *kun rdzob la gnyis kyi/ log pa'i kun rdzob sngar dang 'dra/ yang dag kun rdzob ni/ cir snang ba thams cad chos nyid rtogs pa'i byin rlabs rdo rje dbyings kyi dkyil 'khor du snang ba'i phyir/ skye bos snang ba rang rgyud du rtags pa'di med par 'dod do/* "As for the relative truth, there are two: the mistaken relative is just like before. As for the authentic relative: generally, since all appearances by the blessing of realizing the intrinsic nature manifest as the maṇḍala of the indestructible basic sphere, the appearances imputed by ordinary individuals as possessing their own continuum are asserted to be nonexistent."

The Nyingma Khenchen Padma Sherab expressed the view that the relative truth, as set forth in the Nyingma esoteric teachings, can be regarded as equal to the ultimate truth propagated in the dialectical vehicle, and that this is hinted at in Lochen's definition of the relative categories within Yogatantra. (Oral communication, Boudhanath, Spring, 2004)

68 The *Clear Differentiation of the Three Codes*, 308: *bya spyod rnal 'byor rgyud gsum las/ snang ba lha ru gsungs pa med/* "The three tantras of Kriyā, Caryā, and Yoga do not teach that appearances are to be perceived as divine." See also ibid., 309: *de na kun rdzob ldog pa dang/ lha yi ldog pa ma phyed pas/ gsang sngags rnying ma'i kun rdzob kun/ lta ba dang 'khrul de ltar yin/* (translation by Rhoton in Sakya Pandita (2002): 132): "This is how the entire conventional reality of the Old School of Mantra has been confused with the theory, because the aspect of conventional appearances has not been differentiated from that of deities." Sapaṇ criticizes the Nyingma approach, in the context of the lower tantras, of regarding phenomena as pure even on the conventional level, and thus failing to properly differentiate between view and meditation as well as between method (*upāya*) and wisdom (*prajñā*).

In a recent conversation with Khenpo Ape (Yon tan bzang po) of the Sakya school, he similarly suggested to me that a discrepancy exists between the Nyingma school and the Gelug and Sakya schools, in that the Nyingma explain that relative appearances are already pure on the level of the three lower tantras, while the other two schools claim that there is still a differentiation between pure and impure. (Oral communication, Boudhanath, November, 2003)

69 I would therefore disagree with Pettit who surmises that in the Nyingma school, "the last three are called 'inner tantras' (*nang rgyud*) and are considered equivalent to the anuttarayogatantras of the new traditions." (Pettit (1999): 63)

70 For a discussion on Longchen Rabjam's project of aligning the Nyingma tantras with the tantras of the New Schools, see Germano (1994).

71 As pointed out in Germano (1994): 247, n. 114.

72 *Collected Works of Rongzom*, vol. 1, 294.

73 *Collected Works of Rongzom*, vol.1, 337. However, Rongzom's use of the terms "the way of generation" (*skyed pa'i tshul*), "the way of perfection" (*rdzogs pa'i tshul*), and "the way of great perfection" (*rdzogs pa chen po'i tshul*) cannot be taken as an indication that the terms Mahā, Anu, and Ati yoga were later constructions, for in some Tunhuang documents these terms are already frequently used with reference to the higher tantras. See for instance Tsuda (1965).

74 *Collected Works of Rongzom*, vol.1, 502: *yo ga ni spyod pa blang dor dang yang ldan la/ bsam pa lha dang bdag gnyis su'ang byed do/ ma h'a yo ga ni de las bzlog pa'o// a nu yo ga ni rjes su mthun pa'i rnal 'byor ces bya ste/ dbyings dang ye shes gnyis su med pa'i rig pa skad cig ma gcig la/ lta spyod thams cad rdzogs par 'dod pas/ a ti yo ga dang rjes su mthun te/ cung zad brtsal* (sic) *ba dang bral bar la ma zlos pas rjes su mthun pa'i rnal 'byor zhes bya'o//* "In Yoga, the conduct is still immersed in acceptance and rejection, while mentally there is the dualism of oneself and the deity. Mahāyoga is free of that. Anuyoga is called the concordant Yoga. Since it is asserted that in the awareness of nondual basic space and wisdom [all aspects of] view and conduct are perfected in a single instant, this accords with Atiyoga. Since [Anuyoga] does not resolve [the view and conduct] beyond [the application of] slight effort, it is called 'concordant Yoga.'"

75 *Collected Works of Rongzom*, vol. 1, 332-333: *rnal 'byord phyi pa thub pa rgyud ces bya ba la/ phyi pa ni mdor bsdu' na lta spyod gnyis kyi sgo nas phyir gzhag ste/ de la lta bas kund rdzob tu bdag dang sang rgyas mnyam par mi lta ba dang/ spyod pas mnyam pa'i brtul zhugs dang du mi len pa'o/ thub pa ni brsung du myed pa'i dam tshig nyams su len mi nus te/ thun mong gi sdom pa rnams dang ma bral ba'o/ nang pa' thabs kyi rgyud ces bya ba ni/ de las bzlog pa'* (sic) *nyid yin te/ bdag nyid ma nor ba'i dbang phyug chen por lta ba dang/ mnyam pa'i brtul zhugs dang du len pa dang/ sgo gsum gyi spyod pa la bkag pa myed kyang skyon kyis mi gos pas na thabs mkhas pa'o//*

76 While the Nyingma scholar Lochen Dharma Śrī applies the term "superior" (*lhag pa*) to the two truths in the Mahāyoga context (see, e. g., *Speech of the Lord of Secrets* (*Gsang bdag*), 28a), Rongzom himself does not use this term.

77 *Treasury of Philosophical Tenets*, 254b: *dang po ni lta ba'i khyad la/ phyi pas bden pa so sor 'dod la/ nang pas dbyer med du 'dod do// sgom pa'ang phyi pas lha zhal* (sic) *sbyor mi sgom la nang pas sgom pa'o// spyod pa'ang phyi pas gtsang sbra spyod cing sha lnga la sogs bsten par mi nus la/ nang pas nus pa'o//*

78 *Collected Works of Rongzom*, vol. 1, 502: *gsang sngags kyi nang gi bye brag kyang/ bden pa gnyis dpyer myed par 'dod pa'i dang po kri ya nas brtsams nas/ rdzogs pa chen por mthar phyin to//*

79 *Sbrul nag po'i stong thun.*
80 The inseparability of the two truths is a prominent feature of the Mahāyoga, and some scholars have argued that in the early stages of Buddhism in Tibet Mahāyoga appears to be a synonym for Mantra *in toto*. See for instance Eastman (1983). Thus when Rongzom and Longchen Rabjam, the two paramount masters of the "Early Translations," differentiate between the view of Sūtra and Mantra with reference to the inseparability of the two truths, this might provide a clue as to how the different classifications of Tantra were applied during the Early Dissemination and in particular whether the Mahāyoga, as the principal esoteric class, was at times treated as equivalent with the general category of Mantra set apart from Sūtra. Alternatively, Longchen Rabjam's statement above could indicate a shift in Nyingma exegesis away from considering the external tantras generally capable of realizing the inseparability of the two truths.
81 Longchenpa, a paramount master of the Nyingma tradition, differentiates the Pāramitā vehicle from Mantra in terms of whether or not there is reliance on arguments (*Treasury of Philosophical Tenets*, 206b). This seems rather peculiar when considering that, according to Nyingma tradition, the view of Mahāyoga is also to be realized with the help of arguments (*gtan tshigs*). More research is needed to determine the nature and scope of the esoteric arguments.
82 They are respectively 1. *rgyu gcig pa'i gtan tshigs*, 2. *yig 'bru'i tshul gyi gtan tshigs*, 3. *byin gyis brlabs pa'i gtan tshigs*, and 4. *mngon sum pa'i gtan tshigs* (see *Treasury of Knowledge*, vol. 2, 740-741). Padmasambhava, Rongzom, and Longchenpa refrain from applying the term "arguments" (*gtan tshigs*) to the four realizations (*rtogs pa bzhi*) in their commentaries on the *Guhyagarbha*. Mipham, who in the *Survey of the Guhyagarbha Tantra* joins Jamgon Kongtrul in referring to them as arguments (*gtan tshigs*), elaborates on his reasons for doing so by stating that since they unfailingly allow one to gain access to the profound view of Mantra, they are to be termed "arguments." (Mipham (2000): 466)
83 See *Treasury of Knowledge*, vol. 2, 741-743.
84 *Gsang sngags bka' yi tha ram.*
85 Nyang ral nyi ma 'od zer.
86 Sakya Pandita (2002): 308: *rnal 'byor chen po'i rgyud du ni dag pa gsum gyi rang bzhin bshad 'di yi lung rigs man ngag rnams bla ma'i zhal las legs par dris.*
87 The term "argument" (*gtan tshigs*) appears in the Mantrayāna treatises of the two Kathog hierarchs Dampa Desheg (Dam pa bde gshegs) and his disciple Tsangton Dorje Gyaltsen (Gtsang ston rdo rje rgyal mtshan). James Gentry (who has provided me with these references) suggests that the use of tantric arguments was a defining feature of the Zur tradition. He supports this hypothesis with reference to Yungton Dorje Pal's (G.yung ston rdo rje dpal) systematic use of argument in the third and eleventh chapter of his *Guhyagarbha* commentary based on the Zur tradition, *Mirror Illuminating the Guhyagarbha Tantra* (*Gsang snying rgyud don gsal byed me long*).
88 *Speech of the Lord of Secrets*, 28a: *gong ma rnams/ kun rdzob lam du byed nus pa dang mi nus pa'i khyad par yod par bzhad de/ pha rol tu phyin pas don dam bsgrub bya dang/ kun rdzob spang byar byed la/ sngags las ni kun rdzob tu'ang chos tams chad la mnyam pa nyid du spyod pas na/ mi spong bar lam du byed pa'i phyir/ bden gnyis phyogs su ma lhung pas 'phags te/*

89 Mipham makes a similar differentiation (*Survey of the Guhyagarbha Tantra*, 424): *des na mdo lam na kun rdzob tu 'khor 'das spang blang du byed cing/ 'dir 'khor 'das dbyer med mnyam par sbyor ba'i tshul gyis lam la 'jug pa yin no//* "Therefore, on the path of Sūtra, saṃsāra and nirvāṇa are on the relative level rejected and accepted; [yet], here [in Mantra] one enters the path through joining within equality saṃsāra and nirvāṇa as inseparable."

90 This absence of an object of refutation (*dgag bya, pratiṣedhya*) allows for the inseparability of the two truths: if the ultimate is achieved through negating relative truth, the inseparability or unity of the two truths is precluded. Rongzom seems to have been very skeptical of an approach which ascribes a greater veridical value—and thus a measure of objectivity—to the authentic relative truth (*yang dag pa'i kun rdzob*) than to the deceptive (*log pa'i kun rdzob*), while the same properties of authentic relative truth are exclusively negated in the context of the ultimate.

91 *Precious Wish-fulfilling Treasury*, 251a: *'bras bu sangs rgyas sgrub par don gcig na'ang/ sgrub tshul la rmongs ma mongs kyi khyad par yod de/ mtshan nyid las/ phyi snang ba'i bden zhen bszlog pa la sgyu ma sgom pa la sogs pas 'byung ba'i rig pa la rmongs/ nang phung po lhar ma shes pas gnas pa'i don la rmongs/ gsang ba rtog tshogs dang nyon mongs pa ye shes su ma shes pas lam gyi rnam pa la rmongs/ thams cad dag nyams bden pa dbyer med du ma shes pas rtogs pa'i lta ba la rmongs pa nyid/* "Although the [Sūtra and Mantra approaches] are identical in accomplishing the result, Buddhahood, they can be differentiated in terms of whether there is a presence of obscuration regarding the way of accomplishing [that result]. The dialectical [vehicle] is obscured in terms of the awareness ensuing [from the application of the path] because [in that vehicle] for instance one meditates on illusion in order to remedy the apprehension of truth in outer appearances. Since one does not know the inner skandhas to be divinities, it is obscured in terms of the abiding object, and since on the innermost level the mass of conceptual thoughts and negative emotions are not known to be primordial wakefulness, it is obscured in terms of the features of the path. Since the inseparability of the two truths within everything being pure equality is not understood, it is indeed obscured in terms of the view to be realized."

92 *Treasury of Philosophical Tenets*, 208b: *mtshan nyid pa lta ba stong nyid spros bral tsam las/ bden pa dbyer med gdod ma nas lha dang sngags kyi rang bzhin gnas par ma rtogs la/ sngags kyis rtogs te/*

93 The *Clear Differentiation of the Three Codes*, 308: *pha rol phyin pa'i spros bral las/ lhag pa'i lta ba yod na ni/ lta de spros pa can du 'gyur/ spros bral yin na khyad par med/*

"If there would be a view higher than
The freedom from all mental constructs of the Pāramitā vehicle,
This view would become possessed by [mental] constructs.
If they [all] are free of [mental] constructs,
They are without difference."

94 We may note that Śakya Chogden (Śa kya mchog ldan) (1428-1507) here takes Sapaṇ to be speaking of the view as established through learning and reflecting, and not of the view *qua* object of direct experience. Śakya Chogden furthermore proposes the existence of a tantric Madhyamaka, which he equates with the views set forth in the tantras and which he considers higher than the sūtric Madhyamaka. See Komarovski (2000).

95 Ibid., 309: *des na thos pa'i lta ba ni/ dbu ma yan chad thams cad mthun/*

96 *Beacon of Certainty*, 50: *spros bral dbu ma chen po dang/ od gsal rdzogs pa chen po gnyis/ don gcig ming gi rnam grangs te/ de las lhag pa'i lta ba med/ gang phyir snang stong res 'jog tu// 'dzin med mtha' bzhi'i spros pa dang/ bral phyir de las gzhan gyur na/ spros dang mcas pa nyid phyir ro//* In the same text Mipham explains, "To resolve decisively primordial purity, one must perfect the Prāsaṅgika view. It is said that from the point of view of the freedom from [mental] constructs, [Tantra and Prāsaṅgika] are without difference. To avert the grasping at emptiness the tantras teach great bliss." *ka dag bdar sha chod pa la/ thal 'gyur lta ba mthar phyin dgos// spros bral tsam gyi cha nas ni/ de nyis khyad par med do gsungs/ stong par zhen pa zlog phyir du/sngags las bde ba chen po bstan//* (*Beacon of Certainty*, 19). For Mipham, the Prāsaṅgika approach constitutes a crucial step in the approach of the Great Perfection. Mipham minimizes the difference between his versions of Madhyamaka and Mantrayāna and yet suggests that Tantra has more to offer than Madhyamaka. The teaching of great bliss or, as it is also referred to, luminosity (*'od gsal*), provides an antidote to grasping at emptiness. Thus, freedom from mental constructs (*spros bral, niṣprapañca*) is by no means resonant with nothingness, and its very realization can be achieved by acknowledging the central messages of Mantrayāna.

97 We may conclude that Mipham interprets Madhyamaka from a decidedly tantric perspective. We shall return to this issue in chapter 3, where Rongzom's view of Madhyamaka will be compared with that of Mipham.

98 Mipham generally differentiates the view of Mantra from that of Sūtra with reference to the subject's realization. That is, the object realized, the *dharmadhātu* beyond mental constructs, remains the same in both Sūtra and Mantra. The difference between the two can and should, however, be determined with reference to the mind that realizes that single object of realization, the *dharmadhātu*. In the *Survey of the Guhyagarbha Tantra* (436), Mipham explains that in the Nyingma tantras three types of views are differentiated: (1) the view that regards the object (*chos can lta ba'i lta ba*), (2) the view that regards the intrinsic nature (*chos nyid lta ba'i lta ba*), and (3) the view that regards original awareness (*rang rig lta ba'i lta ba*). Furthermore, Mipham states that they are synonyms for respectively: 1. the conventional subject (*tha snyad kyi yul can*), 2. the ultimate subject (*don dam pa'i yul can*), and 3. the subject that [found] certainty in the inseparability of the two truths (*bden gnyis dbyer med par nges pa'i yul can*). A few lines further (*Survey of the Guhyagarbha Tantra*, 437) Mipham clearly states, *gzhal bya chos dbyings spros bral du gtan la 'bebs pa tsam la khyad med kyang/ chos dbyings mthong tshul gyi yul can la khyad yod la/ lta ba ni yul can gyi ngos nas 'jog pas na khyad shin tu che'o//* "Although there is no difference [between Sūtra and Mantra] in terms of merely resolving the object of evaluation, *dharmadhātu* free from [mental constructs], there is a difference in the way the subject perceives *dharmadhātu*. When positing the view from the perspective of the subject, there is an immense difference [between Sūtra and Mantra]."

99 *Differentiation of Views and Tenets*, 86: *mdo sngags kyi lta ba'i khyad par de dang de yi gnad gsang mthar thug pa'i don ni/ lta ba zab mo snang stong 'gal med mchog gi khyad par zung 'jug mtha' bral chen po'i don rim gyi gtan la 'bebs pa dang/ rim min cig char du rdzogs tshul las gyur pa legs so//*

100 Although Tsongkhapa often empasizes that the view of Tantra is nothing but

Madhyamaka, he nevertheless also suggests that the subject realizing emptiness is different from the Sūtrayāna subject in that realization. Tsongkhapa describes the subject in the esoteric context as great bliss (*bde ba chen po, mahāsukha*). See for instance Komarovski (2000): 73, n. 103.

101 *Sngags rim chen mo.*

102 *The Stages of Mantra* (*Snags rim chen mo*), 20-21: *spyir theg pa che chung stong pa nyid kyi shes rab kyis mi 'byed par thabs kyis 'byed dgos la/ khyad par du theg pa chen po la gnyis su phye ba yang zab mo rtogs pa'i shes rab kyis mi 'byed kyi/ thabs kyis dbye dgos . . .*

Lopez observes, "Thus, for Tsongkhapa, there is no difference in the profundity of the highest wisdom in Sūtra and Tantra. The superiority of the Tantric vehicle must therefore be found in the domain of method." (Lopez (2000): 524)

103 Lessing and Wayman (1983): 92: */sngags kyi rgyud sde thams cad kyi lta ba thal 'gyur ro//* Khedrup later indicates that Nāgārjuna likewise did not assert the view of Tantra being higher than that of Madhyamaka (334).

104 For instance, Do-ngag Tenpay Nyima (*Differentiation of Views and Tenets*, 83) describes appearance as the aspect of luminosity: *'on kyang snang cha nas gzhal na/ dpal ma h'a yo ga'i lugs kyi snang cha 'od gsal ba'i rang bzhin kun 'rdzob dag pa chen po'i lta ba dang/ a nu yo ga'i lta ba snang cha nas kun tu bzang po gdan gsum lha yi dkyil 'khor a ti yo ga'i lta ba zab mo gzhi snang lhun grub kyi dkyil 'khor rnams ni mtshan nyid theg par ming yang ma grags pas na mdo sngags kyi lta ba'i khyad par gnam sa tsam yod par.* "However, if you were to analyze from the standpoint of appearances, then according to the tradition of the glorious Mahāyoga, the appearance aspect is the nature of luminosity, the relative truth, the view of great purity. According to the view of Anuyoga, the appearance aspect is Samantabhadra, the maṇḍala of the three divine seats, and according to the profound view of Atiyoga, [the appearance aspect] is the ground appearances, the spontaneously accomplished maṇḍala. Since even such terms [not to mention their meaning] are unknown in the dialectical vehicle, the difference between Sūtra and Mantra is simply [as vast as that] between heaven and earth."

105 See for instance Karmay (1988) and Wangchuk (2002).

106 This argument is contrary to John Pettit's, for instance, who states that the main reason for Mipham and Rongzom to comment on the *Garland of Views as Oral Instructions* was their intention to harmonize the Great Perfection with the highest view of the dialectical vehicle, epitomized by Madhyamaka. See Pettit (1999): 86. Although Padmasambhava in the *Garland of Views as Oral Instructions* uses the term Madhyamaka (*dbu ma*) to describe the view of the higher tantras, we cannot take the simple fact that Rongzom chose to write a commentary on the *Garland of Views as Oral Instructions* as evidence that he tried to harmonize the Great Perfection with Madhyamaka. His other treatises abound with criticism of the Madhyamaka.

107 See below, chapter 3.3.

108 See Hayes (1994).

109 See Dreyfus and McClintock (2003).

110 While the general consensus came to term the supreme view "Prāsaṅgika," scholars differed widely in how they defined that view. For excellent discussions of this subject, see Dreyfus and McClintock (2003). Tsongkhapa, for instance, in the four-

teenth century became a fierce promoter of what he termed Prāsaṅgika and contributed greatly to the domination of the Prāsaṅgika view. However, before Tsongkhapa's strong propagation of Prāsaṅgika-Madhyamaka, Longchen Rabjam already clearly preferred his version of Prāsaṅgika over the Svātantrika. See chapter 12 of Longchen Rabjam's *Precious Wish-fulfilling Treasury.*

111 *Collected Works of Rongzom*, vol. 2, 20-21: *don dam par skye 'gag med par 'dod pa ni dbu ma dang mthun no/ kun rdzob tu phung po khams dang skye mched sgyu ma tsam du lta ba'ang mthun no/ bye brag tu na sgyu ma'i mtshan nyid de dag kyang yongs su dag pa'i lha'i mtshan nyid du lta ba dang/ bden pa gnyis kyang dbyer med par lta bas bye brag tu byas pa'//*

112 *Speech of Delight*, 116: *rnam grangs pa'i don dam khas len dang bcas pa de rtsal du bton nas 'chad pa rang rgyud pa'i mtshan nyid yin la/ rnam grangs ma yin pa'i don dam khas len kun bral rtsal du bton nas 'chad pa thal 'gyur ba yin pa shes par bya'o//*

113 See *Speech of Delight*, 62.

114 *Collected Works of Rongzom*, vol. 1, 323: *de la rnam grangs kyi don dam pa ni/ spros pa'i phyogs re chad pa dang/ phyogs re ma chad pa'i blo'i yul te/ 'di' ltar stong pa nyid bco' brgyad las stsogs pa/ don dam pa'i rnam grangs kyi tshig gis bstan par bya ba'i tshig gi don rnams so// spros pa dang bral ba'i don dam pa ni/ spros pa thams cad yongs su zhi ba'i rang bzhin gang yin pa'o//* While we find the term "severed" (*chad pa*) in Rongzom's definition of the figurative, this term is absent in the definition of the nonfigurative. Rongzom does not consider exclusion or negation essential for a final understanding of the ultimate.

115 For Mipham the figurative ultimate is an existential negation (*med dgag, prasajya-pratiṣedha*) and, as such, still a conceptual construct. Existential negation is distinguished from predicative negation (*ma yin dgag, paryudāsa*) in that, in predicative negation, the affirmation of some property or entity other than the negated is implied by the negation itself. Existential negation is ultimate in that it leaves nothing implicitly affirmed. On the two negations in Indian Buddhism, see Kajiyama (1973).

116 *Collected Works of Rongzom*, vol. 2, 18: *de yang don dam pa'i lta ba mthun yang kun rdzob kyi bye brag gis/ mdo sde dbu ma dang/ rnal 'byor spyod pa'i dbu ma gnyis su gyes* (sic) *so/* The same classification is found in anonymous textual fragments found at Tunhuang (see Lang (1990): 130 and n. 12). Yeshe De (Ye shes sde) (ca. 800) in his *Differentiation of Views* (*lta ba'i khyad par*) mentions Bhāvaviveka and Śāntarakṣita as representatives of these two classifications (see Tauscher (1995): 6, n. 7).

117 Dreyfus in his article "Would the True Prāsaṅgika Please Stand?" states that "Rongzom had a clear preference for Śāntarakṣita's view, which he described as Yogācāra-Madhyamaka and contrasted favorably with Bhāvaviveka's Sautrāntika-Madhyamaka." Thus, Dreyfus concludes, "for Rong-zom, it is the view that came to be classified later as Yogācāra-Svātantrika-Madhyamaka that is to be preferred in the context of the Great Perfection." (Dreyfus (2003): 331) However, no evidence supports a perceived compatibility with Dzogchen as a reason for Rongzom to hold Yogācāra-Madhyamaka superior to the Sautrāntika-Madhyamaka. In the context of the passage cited, Rongzom simply states the classifications of Madhyamaka that were used in his day, remarking without any reference to Dzogchen that he prefers the Yogācāra-Madhyamaka interpretation.

118 See for instance Tauscher (2003): 209.

119 See Lang (1990).

120 See *Collected Works of Rongzom,* vol. 2, 20: *dbu ma'i lta ba mdor bsdus na/ ma ya ste sgyu ma lta bu 'dod pa dang/ a bra ti sti te rab tu mi gnas par 'dod pa'o//* Ruegg mentions that Advayavajra (eleventh century) divided Madhyamaka into Māyopamādvayavādins and Sarvadharmāpratiṣṭhānavādins (Ruegg (1981): 58). Rongzom refers to the same subschools using both the Sanskrit names and their Tibetan translations.

121 Sapaṇ, for example, divides the Sarvadharmāpratiṣṭhānavādins further into Prāsaṅgika and Svātantrika; see Tauscher (1995): 6 and n. 9. When describing the commentarial tradition relying on Nāgārjuna, Tsongkhapa presents briefly some opinions of earlier scholars regarding the divisions of Madhyamaka, and indicates that to him these divisions are not acceptable. Later commentators on Tsongkhapa's particular viewpoint disagree on whether he implied that the earlier scholars misinterpreted the relevant assertions of Sarvadharmāpratiṣṭhānavādins and Māyopamādvayavādins, or whether he meant that their identification of Sarvadharmāpratiṣṭhānavādins with Prāsaṅgika and Māyopamādvayavādins with Svātantrika is incorrect (see Napper (1989): 403-404).

122 See Tillemans (2003).

123 According to the higher esoteric teachings there is nothing to be abandoned since everything is already pure. Secondly, there are no distinctions to be made with regard to either false or true phenomena, for everything is great equality.

124 *Collected Works of Rongzom,* vol. 1, 434-435.

125 See Tillemans (2003).

126 *Collected Works of Rongzom,* vol. 1, 422.

127 *Collected Works of Rongzom,* vol. 1, 423: *'di lta bu bsgrub pa ni chus khyer ba rtsa drungs byung la 'ju' ba dang 'dra'o/ de la 'di skad du/ don dam par bsgrub par bya ba mi 'dod na/ kun rdzob tsam ni ma brtags na nyams dga' ba/ brtags na rigs pa'i spungs mi bzod pa yin pas/ rigs pas gnod pa la 'gal ba myed do zhe na/ 'o na kun rdzob du bsgrub pa tsam la rigs pa mi dgos pa zhig na/ snang du 'dra yang don byed nus pa dang mi nus pa'i bye brag gis yang dag pa dang yang dag pa ma yin par rnam par gzhag go zhes pa de nyid rigs pa ma yin nam/ 'di ltar yang dag par sgrub kyang rung/ re shig tsam du sgrub kyang rung ste/ rang rang gi sa tshad tsam sgrub par byed pa'i rig pa'i spungs tsam yang mi bzod na/ tha snyad tsam yang ji ltar 'grub par gyur/ dper na dgra'i dpung 'joms par byed pa'i glang po che la dpung gi tshogs khur nas tho ba'i lcags kyis bskul ba'i spungs bzod pa lta bu ma yin du zin kyang/ zhing tsam rmo ba'i bya ba byed pa'i ba la'ang gnya' shing khur nas/ 'khri shing gi lcag gis bskul ba'i spungs tsam yang mi bzod na/ zhing rmo ba'i bya ba byed ces bya ba'i tha snyad kyang ji ltar 'jug ste/ ra skyes kyi spungs dang bye brag du gyur pa ci zhig yod/*

128 *Collected Works of Rongzom,* vol. 1, 423: *yang dag pa'i kun rdzob ces kyang ji ltar tha snyad 'jug ste/ 'jig rten phal pa'i lta ba dang bye brag du gyur pa ci zhig yod/ 'di lta bu'i lta ba ya bral 'chang ba di ni/ shin tu ngo mtshar ba'i gnas yin no//*

129 *Collected Works of Rongzom,* vol. 1, 424: *chos thams cad don dam par spros pa thams cad nye bar zhi ste/ bsgrub par bya ba gang yang mi sgrub par lta bzhin du/ yang dag pa'i kun rdzob kyi mtshan nyid spang ba dang blang bar bya ba'i rdzas yod par 'dzin pa de ni/ shin tu mi tsham pa 'dzin pa ste ngo mtshar ba'i gnas yin no//*

130 *Collected Works of Rongzom,* vol. 1, 425: *bsgrub par bya ba'i chos gang yang myed par rtogs pa na/ don thams cad myed par 'go mnyam mo//*

131 *Collected Works of Rongzom,* vol. 2, 69: *kho bo cag ni khyad cag gi lta ba ngan pa zlog*

pa tsam ste/ lhag par don ci yang mi sgrub bo/ de la tha snyad du mnyam pa chen po'i lta ba zhes 'dogs te/ lta bar zhen pa ni gang yang med do//

132 *Collected Works of Rongzom,* vol. 1, 460: *dbu ma pa chos rnams rang bzhin myed pa nyid yin par 'dod pa la/ . . . 'on kyang bden pa gnyis kyi blo mi 'dor bas/ gnyis su myed par lta ba'i grangs su mi chud de/*

133 *Speech of Delight,* 114-122. Dreyfus remarks on Mipham's Prāsaṅgika, "Objective existence is negated by the Prāsaṅgika, according to Mipham, because it involves the provisional separation of the two truths and the assertion of the objective validity of the conventional." (Dreyfus (2003): 336).

134 *Collected Works of Rongzom,* vol. 1, 422: *gang gi tshe yang dag par bsgrub par bya ba zhig yod par 'dod pa de'i tshe ni/ kun rdzob kyi bye brag ji snyed du dbye ba thams cad kyang de bzhin du bsgrub tu rung bar 'gyur la/ gang gi tshe yang dag par sgrub par bya ba zhig bsgrub tu myed par 'dod pa de'i tshe/ kun rdzob kyi bye brag thams cad 'go mnyam par 'gyur ro//*

135 *Collected Works of Rongzom,* vol. 2, 66-68.

136 The four types of *yod pa* (*bhāva*) are 1. *kun rdzob tu yod pa,* 2. *rdzad su yod pa,* 3. *btags su yod pa,* and 4. *don dam par yod pa.*

137 *Collected Works of Rongzom,* vol. 1, 327: *dbu ma pa ni kun rdzob kyi bden pa/ yongs su ma dag pa'i mtshan nyid kyi spyod yul la mngon par zhen pa'o/*

138 See, e.g., *Speech of Delight,* 114-116.

139 Cf. ibid., 76-78, 116, 604-606.

140 Khro shul 'jam rdor.

141 Pettit (1999): 389.

142 *Speech of Delight,* 84.

143 See, e.g., *Speech of Delight,* 56-58.

144 According to Mahāyoga the relative truth consists of great purity (*dag pa chen po*). See chapter 2.1.

145 *Beacon of Certainty,* 5: *'phags yul dpal ldan zla ba dang/ bod na rong zom chos bzang gnyis/ dgongs pa gcig dang dbyangs gcig gis/ ka dag stong pa chen po bsgrubs/ chos 'di ka nas dag pa'am/ gdod nas rang bzhin med pa'i phyir/ bden pa gnyis char ma skyes pas/*

146 *Speech of Delight,* 84.

147 Candrakīrti classically asserts so in *Madhyamkāvatāra* VI, 38.

148 Primordial purity (*ka dag*), a principle presented in Atiyoga, is distinguished from the purity (*dag pa*) taught as the relative truth in Mahāyoga and from the "complete purity" (*rnam dag*) used in the context of Atiyoga. Germano remarks, "Ka Dag is a neologism only found in Great Perfection works, which literally means pure (Dag) from the letter 'A,' Ka being the first letter of the Tibetan alphabet . . . Longchenpa consistently explains this 'original purity' as referring to emptiness (sTong Pa Nyid)." (Germano (1992): 914-915)

149 Tibetan text on p. 115.

150 While Mipham at times extols the virtues of the gradual Svātantrika approach that characteristically operates by making distinct claims regarding the two truths, he makes it clear that in the final analysis all such claims will necessarily be transcended (see, e.g., *Speech of Delight,* 504).

151 The Madhyamaka being considered the highest philosophical school within the Sūtra system.

152 *Ketaka Jewel,* 3b.

153 In the thirteenth century Dzogchen came under attack for being similar to the suddenist path of the Chinese teacher Mo Ho Yen, who purportedly was defeated in debate by the Indian master Kamalaśīla and expelled from the Tibetan empire in the eighth century. While the ordinances of Lha Lama Yeshe Ö and Photreng Shiway Ö do not propose any similarity between Dzogchen and the teachings of Mo Ho Yen, Davidson suggests that anti-Chinese polemics were introduced for the first time in Sapaṇ's *Clear Differentiation of the Three Codes* (Davidson (2002): 208). Rongzom may therefore not have felt any need to defend Dzogchen against a perceived similarity with Ch'an. Mipham, on the other hand, sets his exposition of nonconceptuality (*rnam par mi rtog pa*) explicitly apart from the view of Mo Ho Yen (*Speech of Delight*, 104).

154 Although Rongzom could be seen as a radical antirealist because of his opposition to an objective relative reality, one may wonder whether his view might not be more accurately considered a form of metaphysical realism, since he classifies purity as relative truth. Granting that type of veridical status to purity could be seen as providing it with a solid ontological grounding in a transcendental reality. However, given Rongzom's continuous objections to any form of ontological foundationalism, be it at the relative or ultimate level, I hesitate to classify Rongzom's view as metaphysical realism.

155 This is suggested by Dreyfus (2003): 318.

156 On the *Śrāvakabhūmi*'s use of the four reasonings, see Yoshimizu (1996): 160.

157 *Mkhas pa'i tshul la 'jug pa'i mgo.*

158 *Don rnam par nges pa shes rab ral gri.*

159 Karma Phuntsho, *Steps to Valid Cognition,* 227-233.

160 Ibid., 227: *de la rigs pa zhes pa ni nya' ya zhes bya ba nya'a ya ste/ rang bzhin nam tshul la'ang 'jug pas dngos po'i rang bzhin ji ltar gnas pa la rigs pa zhes bya'o// yang yuk ti ste chos dang ldan pas rigs pa zhes bya'o//*

161 Ibid.: *chos rnams kyi rang bzhin de ltar gnas pa ni 'od shing rigs pa nyid kyi phyir rigs pa zhes brjod pa'am/ de dang mthun par gzhal ba la rigs pa zhes brjod pa yin no//* Likewise, Kapstein observes *rigs pa* to have psychological, as well as extra-mental, connotations, a usage which, he remarks, is also common in the English use of "reason." (Kapstein (2001): 322)

162 Yoshimizu (1996): 160. In Jamgon Kongtrul's renowned *Treasury of Knowledge,* the four principles of reasoning are classified as hermeneutical tools that may be used in common to interpret Sūtra texts as well Mantra. However Kapstein wonders whether the inclusion of the four principles as tools for scriptural interpretation could be a mere classificatory accident. See Kapstein (2001): 322. These principles point to differing levels of reality and they bear ontological connotations that are much stronger than their status as hermeneutical means. However the *Saṁdhinirmocanasūtra* provides, probably for the first time, the method for examining the words of the Buddha through the three investigations (*dpyad pa gsum*), which again could be considered a form of the principle of reasoning of valid proof. See Yoshimizu (1996): 163.

163 Karma Phuntsho, *Steps to Valid Cognition,* 227: *de ltar na don rang rang gi ngang tshul ji ltar gnas pa dang/ de dang mthun pa'i blo gnyis ka la'ang rigs pa'i sgra 'jug pas/ chos kyi mtshan nyid dang de dang mthun pa'i blo gnyis ka la'ang 'jug par shes par bya'o//* I have been unable to identify the exact source for this citation.

164 When explaining the essence of reasoning (*rigs pa*), *Steps to Valid Reasoning* defines it as "the possession of tenability" (*thad pa dang ldan pa*). Reasoning (*rigs pa*) is moreover divided into the "reasoning pertaining to the abiding object" (*gnas pa yul gyi rigs pa*) and the "reasoning pertaining to the subject, the establisher" (*sgrub byed yul can gyi rigs pa*). These two aspects of reasoning, the objective and the subjective, are then subdivided into the four principles of reasoning and we arrive at eight different reasonings by reference to either object cognized or cognizing subject. *Steps to Valid Reasoning*, 231, contains the following remark: *rigs pa brgyad las sgrub byed yul can gyi rigs pa bzhi po thams cad yul la gnas pa'i 'thad pa sgrub pa'i rigs pa'i khong su bsdu ste/ de dag rten 'brel gyi ngang tshul sgrub par byed pa'i rigs pa yin pa'i phyir/ gnas pa yul gyi rigs pa bzhi po yang ngo bo chos nyid kyi rigs pa'i khongs su bsdu ste/* "Among the eight reasonings, all four principles of reasoning pertaining to the subject can be subsumed into the principle of reasoning of valid proof as pertaining to the abiding object. This is so, since they are the reasonings that establish the nature of dependent originations. Moreover, the four principles of reasoning pertaining to the object can all be subsumed into the reasoning of the intrinsic nature."

165 Tibetan text on pp. 114–115.

166 Tibetan text on p. 117.

167 *Collected Works of Rongzom*, vol. 1, 487-488: *rigs pa rnam pa bzhi'i sgo nas gzhal yang/ dngos po lta ba rnams kyi grub mtha' gcig la gcig gnod pa tsam yang dmigs la/ gzhan yang rigs pa nyid thal bar gyur nas slar gnod pa dmigs par zad de/*

168 *Valid Means of Cognition*, 349a: *chos nyid kyi rigs pa zhes bya ba ni/ chos rnams kyi rang bzhin gyi sgo nas brjod pa yin te/ chos rnams la kun rdzob kyi bden pa dang don dam pa'i bden pa gang dang gang gi rang bzhin yod pa de dang de bstan pa'o//*

In *Steps to Valid Reasoning* this reasoning as it pertains to the subjective establisher is set forth in the following way (*Steps to Valid Reasoning*, 230): *Chos rang gi ngo bo gang yin pa sgrub par byed pa'i rigs pa de'i mtshan nyid/* "This is defined as being the reasoning that establishes that which is the essence of the [given] phenomenon itself."

And as it pertains to the abiding object (*Steps to Valid Reasoning*, 229): *chos rnams rang gi thun mong dang thun mong min pa'i ngo bor gnas pa'i rten 'brel gyi ngang tshul de'i mtshan nyid/* "This is defined as being the natural mode of the dependently originating common and uncommon essences of phenomena themselves."

169 *Valid Means of Cognition*, 202b-203a: *kun rdzob kyi bden pa dang/ don dam pa'i bden pa dang/ rnam par dbye ba'i bden pa dang/ nges par rtogs pa'i bden pa dang/ dngos po'i bden pa dang/ nus pa'i bden pa dang/ zad pa dang mi skye ba'i shes pa'i bden pa dang/ lam la 'jug pa'i shes pa'i bden pa dang/ de bzhin shegs pa'i ye shes kun 'byung ba'i bden pa ste/ 'di dag ni bden pa bcu'o//*

170 *Collected Works of Rongzom*, vol. 1, 488: *ngo bo nyid kyi sgo nas sgrub par byed pa ni chos nyid kyi rigs pa.*

171 Ibid., 488: *ngo bo nyid la the tshom za ba.*

172 *Abhidharmasamuccaya*, 103a: *thog ma med pa'i dus nas rang dang spyi'i mtshan nyid gnas pa'i chos rnams la chos nyid du grags pa'o//*

173 *Saṁdhinirmocanasūtra*, 52b : *chos nyid kyi rigs pa ni 'di lta ste/ de bzhin gshegs pa sngar 'jig rten du byung yang rung/ ma byung yang rung ste/ cho nyid gnas pa dang chos kyi dbyings gnas pa gang yin pa de ni chos nyid kyi rigs pa zhes bya'o//*

174 *Speech of Delight*, 324: *ngo bo nyid las byung ba'i dpe nyi shar dang chu bo thur 'bab dang sran zlum tsher ma rno ba sogs so//*

175 Translated according to Kapstein (2000): 321-322.

176 Obviously the notion of the intrinsic nature being emptiness and absence of self would be unacceptable to the Cārvāka materialist, who insists on the exclusive veridical status of what is perceived through the senses.

177 *Collected Works of Rongzom*, vol. 1, 488: *chos nyid kyi rigs pas bsgrub pa thal drags na/ dngos po thams cad mi ldog ste/ mtha' rang bzhin rgyur sma bar 'gyur ro//*

178 Ibid., 488: *de la dngos por sma ba rnams dngos po sgrub pa na/ phal cher chos nyid kyi rigs pa dang mgnon sum gyis sgrub par byed de/de bas na 'di gnyis kyis tshad dang thal ba brjod par bya'o//*

179 I have so far not discovered the same skeptical approach in other texts that treat these principles.

180 Here follows a short overview of the passage in *Collected Works of Rongzom*, vol. 1, 488-489.

181 Although Rongzom differentiates two types of knowledge (*prajñā*), he subsequently seems to refer to the nonconceptual *prajñā* by the term "nonconceptual wisdom" (*rnam par mi rtog pa'i ye shes*).

182 Rongzom finds yet another opportunity here to criticize the authentic relative truth of the Mādhyamikas.

183 *Collected Works of Rongzom*, vol. 1, 489: *de las thal bar gyur na/ dbu ma'i yang dag pa'i kun rdzob dug gis 'chi ba'i chos nyid dang/ sman gyis 'tsho ba'i chos nyid bzhin du/ dngos po rnams kyi chos nyid yin na/ rnal 'byor spyod pa'i sems dang ye shes don dam par yod pa'ang chos nyid du 'gyur/ nyan thos kyi gzung 'dzin dang/ mtha' rang bzhin rgyur lta ba nyid du 'gyur te/ dngos por lta ba thams cad kyi srungs mar 'gyur ro//*

184 Rongzom's criticism of the authentic relative resonates with the Prāsaṅgika approach of Mipham, who highlights Candrakīrti's proclamation of the *svabhāva*-lessness of both truths (as in *Madhyamakāvatāra* VI, 38). Rongzom, in the same passage (*Collected Works of Rongzom,* vol. 1, 489-490), proceeds to demonstrate that direct sense perception (*dbang po'i mngon sum, indriyapratyakṣa*) is delusive.

185 See *Collected Works of Rongzom*, vol. 1, 488-489.

186 Ibid., 488: *chos nyid kyi dngos gzhi la dri ma myed cing dngos gzhi ma log na chos nyid kyi rigs par gzhag du rung ngo/ . . . de la chos nyid kyi dngos gzhi la dri ma yod pa ni/ me shel la tsha ba'i reg pa yod pa lta bu'o/ de la dngos gzhi log pa ni ri dwags me'i gtsang sgra can la me tsha ba'i dngos gzhi log pa lta bu'o//*

187 Not surprisingly, we also find in Rongzom's works uses of intrinsic nature (*chos nyid*) that are more in tune with traditional connotations of *dharmatā qua* the real condition of things.

188 *Shes rab ral gri*, 60: *rigs pa'i mtha' ni chos nyid la/ thug nas rgyu mthsan tsol du med/*

189 Kapstein (2001): 326.

190 Given Mipham's frequent objections to defining the final nature of the ultimate as a negation, it seems unlikely that Kapstein's contrast between things existing conventionally through their defining properties while being devoid of such existence on the absolute level fully captures Mipham's notion of the two aspects of the intrinsic nature.

191 Tibetan text on p. 115.

192 Tibetan text on p. 115. A similar point is made in the *Commentary to the Weapon of Speech* (*Collected Works of Rongzom*, vol. 2, 431).
193 *Collected Works of Rongzom,* vol. 1, 488: *'bras bu'i sgo nas sgrub par byed pa ni bya ba byed pa'i rigs pa.*
194 Tibetan text on p. 116.
195 *Collected Works of Rongzom,* vol. 1, 488: *byed pa la the tsoms za ba.*
196 Ibid., 488: *Bya ba byed pa'i rigs pa thal drags na/ byed pa dang rtsol ba thams cad mi ldog ste/ mtha' byed pa po rgyur smra bar 'gyur ro//*
197 *Saṁdhinirmocanasūtra,* 51a: *chos rnams 'thob pa'am/ 'grub pa'am skyes pa rnams la las byed par 'gyur ba'i rgyu gang dag yin pa dang kyen gang dag yin pa de ni bya ba byed pa'i rigs pa zhes bya'o//*
198 *Abhidharmasamuccaya,* 103a: *gang rang gi mtshan nyid tha dad pa'i chos rnams so sor rang gi bya ba byed pa'o//*
199 *Valid Means of Cognition,* 175a: *bya ba byed pa'i rigs pa zhes bya ba ni las dang rgyu'i sgo nas brjod pa yin te/*
200 *Collected Works of Rongzom,* vol. 1, 488: *rgyu yi sgo nas sgrub par byed pa ni ltos pa'i rigs pa/*
201 *Valid Means of Cognition,* 175a: *chos dang 'bras bu'i rigs pa brjod pa yin te/*
202 *Saṁdhinirmocanasūtra,* 51a: *de la ltos pa'i rigs pa ni 'du byed rnams 'byung ba dang/ rjes su tha snyad dtags pa'i rgyu gang dag yin pa dang rkyen gang dag yin pa ste/*
203 *Abhidharmasamuccaya,* 103a: *gang 'du byed rnams 'byung ba na rkyen la ltos pa'o//*
204 *Collected Works of Rongzom,* vol. 1, 488: *mgon par 'grub pa la the tshom za ba/*
205 Ibid., 488: *ltos pa'i rigs pa thal drags na/ dbangs thams cad mi ldog ste/ mtha' dbangs phyug rgyur smra bar 'gyur ro//*
206 Tibetan text on pp. 116-117.
207 Tibetan text on p. 117.
208 *Collected Works of Rongzom,* vol. 1, 488: *rigs pa nyid dri ma med par byas te sgrub par byed pa ni 'thad pa sgrub pa'i rigs pa'o//*
209 *Abhidharmasamuccaya,* 103a: *gang sgrub pa'i don tshad ma dang mi 'gal bar ston pa'o//*
210 *Valid Means of Cognition,* 175a: *gtan tshigs sgrub pa'i rigs pa zhes bya ba ni/ kun tu 'gro ba yin te/ gang dang gang sgrub pa'i mtshan nyid bstan pa yin no//*
211 *Saṁdhinirmocanasūtra,* 51b: *so so'i shes pa dang/bshad pa dang/ smras pa'i don sgrub pa dang/ legs par khong du chud par bya ba'i rgyu gang dag yin pa dang/ rkyen gang dag yin pa de ni 'thad pa sgrub pa'i rigs pa yin no//*
212 *Collected Works of Rongzom,* vol. 1, 488: *rigs pa la the tshom za ba . . . sel bar byed do//*
213 Ibid., 488: *'thad pa sgrub pa' rigs pa thal drags na/ rigs pa gnas skabs thams cad du dri ma [med par] byed par 'gyur te/ mthar mngon pa'i nga rgyal du 'gyur ro/* In the *Collected Works of Rongzom* this passage lacks the negation that is here kept in square brackets. I have translated according to *Steps to Valid Reasoning,* which features this negation that to me seems necessary for a comprehension of the sentence.
214 Tibetan text on pp. 117-118.
215 This "confinement" refers to the subject's utter lack of experience with *dharmatā,* thus being confined to "this side" (*tshu rol*), as opposed to what is beyond (*pha rol*), saṃsāra.

216 *Survey of the Guhyagarbha Tantra*, 447-448: *de'i phyir na shin tu zab pa'i gnad cung zad bstan na/ kun tu tha snyad pa'i thsad ma la gnyis su yod de/ tshu rol mthong ba la brten pa'i kun tu tha snyad pa'i tshad ma dang/ dag pa'i gzigs pa la brten pa kun tha snyad pa'i tshad ma gnyis su gnas pa'i phyir ro/ de gnyis kyi khyad par cung zad brjod na/ rgyu dang ngo bo byed las 'bras bu'i khyad par bzhi las/ dang po'i rgyu ni rang yul chos can nyi tshe ba la tshul bzhin brtags pa'i stobs las skyes pa'o/ ngo bo rang yul tsam la gnas skabs mi bslu ba'i rigs pa'o/ byed las tshul mthong gi yul la sgro 'dogs sel ba'o/ 'bras bu skabs don yongs su bcad nas 'jug pa'o/ phyi ma'i rgyu chos nyid ji lta ba tshul bzhin dmigs pa'i rjes las thob pa'o/ ngo bo ji snyed pa'i yul can rgya che ba'i shes rab bo/ byed las tha mal pa'i rgyud kyi tshur mthong gis bsam gyis mi khyab pa'i spyod yul la sgro 'dogs sel ba'o// 'bras bu ji snyad mkhyan pa'i ye shes 'grub pa'o//*

217 As the present work explores the ontological and epistemological truth value of the principle of deity in *Establishing Appearances as Divine*, a number of other important topics must, for practical reasons, await a future treatment. These include the notion of purity as it relates to the specific practices of the generation stage (*skyed rim, utpattikrama*), and the various typologies of deities that Rongzom and Mipham discuss.

218 *Differentiation of Views and Tenets*, 107-108: *de bzhin du tha snyad dpyod byed kyi tshad ma yang/ theg dman gyi gzhung spyi dang tshad ma rnam 'grel sogs las bstan pa'i tshul mthong tshad ma tsam las dag gzigs tha snyad pa'i tshad ma 'chad du med pa de'i phyir/ gzhal bya kun rdzob kyang mngon pa'i sde snod las gsung pa ltar gyi gzhi phung khams skye mchad ma dag pa'i kun rdzob 'di tsam las/ rig pa 'dzin pa sngags kyi sde snod las gsungs pa'i gzhi dag pa'i kun rdzob gdan gsum lha yi dkyil 'khor la sogs pa 'grub nus pa min no/ tshul des mdo sngags gnyis ka'i skabs su yang/ don dam med dgag tsam dang/ gzhi'i kun rdzob ma dag pa'i snang ba tsam las lhag pa'i lta ba med pa dang/ gnyug sems 'dus byas su smra ba sogs byung ba yin no//* "Likewise, with respect to conventional valid cognition, the scriptures of the lower vehicle in general and, for instance, the *Pramāṇavārttika,* do not explain the valid cognition of pure vision, but merely the conventional valid cognition of confined seeing. Therefore, also with respect to the relative objects of evaluation, they are merely [able to ascertain the establishment of] the impure relative ground, [the properties of] the aggregates, elements, and sense sources, as laid out in the *Abhidharma piṭaka.* Therefore, they are incapable of [ascertaining] the establishment of the ground [properties of] the pure relative, such as the divine maṇḍala of the three seats taught in the *Mantra piṭaka* of the *vidyādharas.* For such an approach there is, regardless of whether the context is Sūtra or Mantra, moreover no view superior to that of the ultimate being merely an existential negation and the ground [properties] of the relative being merely impure appearances. It will likewise be held, for example, that the intrinsic mind is conditioned."

219 Ibid., 110-111: *tha snyad dag pa'i tshad ma shal gyis bshes pa'i sgo nas/ rgyu mtshan nyid theg pa'i lugs kyi nges don bde gshegs snying po'i snang cha 'od gsal ba'i kun rdzob sogs nas/ dpal ma h'a yo ga'i lugs kyi kun rdzob dag pa chen po nas/ a ti rdzogs pa chen po'i gzhi snang lhun gyis grub pa'i bar gyi kun rdzob dag pa chen po'i rang bzhin 'od gsal ba'i khyad par du byas pa mtha' dag sgro skur dang bral ba sgrub par byed do/ gzhan du dper na tha snyad dag pa'i tshad ma med du zin na/ sgyu 'phrul gsang ba snying po sogs kyi skabs nas bstan pa'i kun rdzob dag pa chen po yod par dam bca' ba tsam las sgrub byed kyi tshad ma mi rnyed de/ don dpyod tshad mas ni de sgrub par mi nus pa tsam du ma zad/ de'i ngor mi stong par yod pa tsam du smrad kyang bden grub tu*

'gyur zhing tshul mthong tshad mas ni phung po lnga ma dag pa dang/ sa sra zhing 'thas pa/ me tsha zhing bsreg pa tsham du 'grub kyi phung lnga rigs lnga dang/ 'byung lnga yum lnga'i dkyil 'khor du bsgrub ga la nus/ "When asserting pure conventional valid cognition, all that which is distinguished by the luminous nature of the great pure relative can be established beyond exaggeration and denigration, beginning with the definitive purport of the dialectical vehicle, such as the relative luminosity, the aspect of appearance of the *sugatagarbha*, [continuing through] the great relative purity of the glorious Mahāyoga, up to and including the spontaneous presence of the ground appearances of Ati, the Great Perfection. Otherwise, if there were no valid cognition of pure conventionality, then for example the existence of the great relative purity as taught in the context of *Mahāmaya Guhyagarbha* would become nothing but a mere thesis and one would fail to find a valid cognition that could prove it. The ultimate valid cognition is incapable of establishing it, and if one were to claim that [great purity] from the perspective of that [ultimate valid cognition] exists as something that is not empty, it would [absurdly] become truly established. As for the valid cognition of confined seeing, this will merely be able to establish the aggregates as impure, earth as solid and supporting, and fire as hot and burning. How could it ever establish the maṇḍala [in which] the five aggregates are the five Buddha families and the five elements the five female Buddhas!"

220 The two conventional ones just explained plus the two ultimate ones that relate to the figurative and nonfigurative ultimate truths (see chapter 3.1).

221 *Differentiation of Views and Tenets*, 202.

222 See, e.g., ibid., 8-9.

223 The tendency of later Nyingma scholars to see Rongzom as an authority on the Svātantrika /Prāsaṅgika distinction is a similar example.

224 See chapter 3.

225 As translated in Pettit (1999): 357.

226 *Beacon of Certainty*, 34: *gnas lugs bden gcig zung 'jug ste/ tshad ma rang byung ye shes nyid/ spang bya ma rig gcig pu las/ med phyir rig dang ma rig tsam/ de phyir tshad ma'i tshul 'di yis/ snang kun rang bzhin lhar sgrub pa/ snga 'ngyur rang lugs kho na ste/ kun mkhyen rong zom paṇḍita'i/ legs bshad seng ge'i nga ro yin/*

227 As translated in Pettit (1999): 212.

228 See for instance Pettit (1999): 217-219. Such a criticism may be directed towards certain Gelug proponents who hold that the divine appearances of the development and completion stages are merely helpful mental creations and as such simply skillful means that have no actual bearing on the abiding condition (*gnas lugs*).

229 *Survey of the Guhyagarbha Tantra*, 418-419: *de ltar rim gnyis lam gyis dri ma bsal stobs kyis gnas tshul mngon du gyur pa yin gyi/ rang bzhin gyis dag pa min na gnas tshul dang 'gal bar yid la byed pa'i bkyed rim dang/ ta mal gyi lus la rlung dgag pa sogs kyis bsgrubs pa'i dngos po rnams rang ngor lha skur shar ba de yang/ sgyu ma'i rde'u la rta glang du snang ba ltar dngos po la mi gnas pa'i 'khrul snang dang/ de 'dzin pa yang log shes su 'gyur zhing/ dug lnga lam du khyer ba dang/ spyod pa blang dor med pa yang tshul de dang 'dra na/ de dra'i lam de mdo las kyang 'phags par khas len pa ni shin tu ya mtshan no/ mdo sngags thabs tsam zhig las lta ba khyad med na bde zhing myur ba'i thabs de mdo las kyang cis mi ston/ des na rgyu'i theg par rgyu 'bras lhun grub tu lta ba med pas thabs de dag kyang re zhig bstan pa'i snod du ma gyur par shes par bya*

zhing/ ye nas dag mnyam chen po'i yin lugs ma shes par thabs tsam shig gis btsan thabs su sems chen sangs rgyas su bsgyur bar sma ba rnams kyis ni/ rim pa gnyis po dngos po'i gnas tsul dang mthun par 'jug pa'i lam du sgrub ma nus par sngags la skur pa chen po btab pa yin par shes par bya'o// In a conversation with Khenpo Ape, the renowned contemporary scholar of the Sakya tradition, he mentioned to me that both Gelug and Sakya believe in transformation (*gnas 'gyur*), the change from impure into pure, on the level of Mantra, while for Nyingmapas there is no actual transformation to be accomplished since everything is already pure from the very outset. This point can be well appreciated with reference to passages such as the above. Mipham here rebukes those who believe in a profound transformation through mere skillful means while their view of reality remains one that apprehends impurity.

230 As noted in the introduction, Rongzom's initial thesis of *Establishing Appearances as Divine* is strikingly similar to Padmasambhava's *Garland of Views as Oral Instructions* (*Collected Works of Rongzom,* vol. 1, 295), where he defines the way of Dzogchen in the following way: *rdzogs pa chen po'i tshul ni/ 'jig rten dang 'jig rten las 'das pa'i chos thams cad dbyer med par sku gsung thugs kyi dkyil 'khor gyi rang bzhin ye nas yin par rtogs nas sgom pa ste/* Later in the same text (297) Padmasambhava explains: *de yang chos thams cad ye nas sang rgyas pa'i rang bzhin du lam gyis bsgrub cing nyen pos bcos su med par rtogs pa'o/ . . . de yang chos thams cad ye nas sang rgyas pa'i rang bzhin yin pas/ bdag nyid kyang ye nas lha rang bzhin yin gyi da lta sgrub pa ni ma yin par rtogs pa'o/* It should also be noted that, as stated in chapter 1, *Establishing Appearances as Divine* is classified by present-day khenpos as a commentary on the *Guhyagarbha Tantra.* If this was Rongzom's intent, his initial thesis and its similarity to Padmasambhava's definition of Dzogchen in his *Garland of Views as Oral Instructions* would lead us to conclude that Rongzom interprets the *Guhyagarbha Tantra* according to Dzogchen. Such a conclusion would correspond with the widely-held opinion of traditional scholars that Rongzom's commentary on the *Guhyagarbha Tantra* assumes a decidedly Dzogchen perspective.

231 Here we note the first imaginary opponent who, in objecting to the primordial enlightenment of all phenomena, may be called a gradualist. As we will see below, Rongzom's opponent is not a non-Buddhist but rather somebody for whom the Mahāyāna sūtras are authorative scriptures.

232 This reply to the opponent is, for me, one of the most enigmatic statements found in *Establishing Appearances as Divine.* Rongzom's thesis is the primordial enlightenment of all phenomena but when confronted with an objection to this thesis, he appears to simply concede that there is nothing but delusion to be found anywhere. How can primordial enlightenment be reconcilable with delusion? Rongzom will elaborate on this intricate issue a few paragraphs below.

233 For a brief discussion of the inseparability of the two truths and whether this inseparability is a unique trait of the higher tantras, see chapter 2.

234 Rongzom, as we will see, emphasizes, along the lines of typical svātantraprayoga, the tenability of the thesis of appearances being pure with reference to there not being different subjects (*chos can, dharmin*) under investigation.

235 Rongzom returns to the puzzling issue of the apparently contradictory claims of primordial enlightenment and omnipresent delusion. It may be rewarding to reflect here on Rongzom's utter dislike for a separation of the two truths, as discussed in

chapter 3. Had Rongzom appealed to the common Buddhist notion of two levels of truth, and simply said that "ultimately all is primordially enlightened, yet on the relative level delusion is a fact," a general Buddhist audience might accept his thesis more readily. Rongzom's unwillingness to confine anything—enlightenment or delusion—to either level of truth describes precisely the approach of the higher tantras, as delineated in chapter 2. While full recourse to the two-truth model would imply a path of gradual transformation from delusion to enlightenment, Rongzom instead bluntly states that the very essence of this all-pervasive experience of delusion is itself enlightenment, and that no other enlightenment could possibly be achieved through a process of purification. As we try to make sense of Rongzom's argument it might be rewarding, despite the anachronism, to consider Mipham's rebuke (pp. 87-88) of those who, while holding phenomena to be in fact impure, nevertheless train in imagining them as pure. Let us also recall the remark of the Sakya Khenchen Ape that the Nyingma school does not believe in transformation (see n. 229). As Nyingma philosophers often espouse this sense of immediacy they can, in this regard, rightly be called suddenists.

236 The term translated as "taken at face value" is the archaic *gzugs por*, which Rongzom uses often in his writings. The translation is, I feel, justified, for in *Entering the Way of the Great Vehicle* (*Collected Works of Rongzom*, vol. 1, 475) Rongzom explains *dgongs pa can* as the opposite of *gzugs por bstan pa*. In the 2001 edition of *Establishing Appearances as Divine*, the term *gzugs por* has been replaced by the word *gzu bor* ("honest, straightforward").

237 The imaginary opponent here appears to be Mahāyānist. In the *Commentary to the Garland of Views as Oral Instructions* (*Collected Works of Rongzom*, vol. 1, 336), Rongzom differentiates between Sūtra and Mantra based on whether or not the subject (*chos can, dharmin*) is regarded as enlightened. It is precisely the Mantrayāna idea of not only *dharmatā* but also the subject being enlightened that the opponent here objects to.

238 See chapter 4 for a description of Rongzom's ambiguity with respect to reasoning.

239 The imaginary opponent thus appears to reveal himself as a proponent of dialectics.

240 For discussion and references regarding the reasoning of the intrinsic nature, see chapter 4.1.

241 On the reasoning of the intrinsic nature being the primary principle of reasoning, see Rongzom's *Commentary to the Weapon of Speech* (*Collected Works of Rongzom*, vol. 2, 431).

242 For a presentation of this reasoning, see chapter 4.2.

243 For a presentation of this reasoning, see chapter 4.3.

244 For a discussion of this issue and a presentation of the reasoning of valid proof, see chapter 4.4.

245 Again, note Rongzom's ambiguity with respect to the value of reasoning, as discussed in chapter 4.

246 The imaginary opponent now appears to be someone generally sympathetic to the tantric thesis of purity.

247 This statement can again be taken as evidence that Rongzom generally addresses an opponent who is a follower of the Mahāyāna.

248 *Viṣayāvatārajñānālokālaṁkārasūtra* (*'phags pa sangs rgyas thams cad kyi yul la 'jug pa'i ye shes snang ba'i rgyan pa'i mdo*). 100 in the *Sde dge* edition of the *Bka' 'gyur.*

249 Thus Rongzom demonstrates the presence of the elements in an autonomous argument (*rang rgyud kyi 'byor ba, svātantraprayoga*).

250 Like Candrakīrti (e.g., *Madhyamakāvatāra* VI, 30), Rongzom refutes the notion of a mundane and yet valid direct perception (*mngon sum, pratyakṣa*), as is evident from *Entering the Way of the Great Vehicle* (*Collected Works of Rongzom,* vol. 1, 490).

251 In establishing all phenomena as "Thus-gone-ones," i.e., purity, based on the evidence that they are unborn, i.e., empty, Rongzom establishes purity with reference to emptiness (*stong pa nyid, śūnyatā*).

252 This could be interpreted as the imaginary opponent agreeing that essentially, or ultimately, phenomena are enlightenment, but doubting whether we may be able to set forth a reasoning that establishes purity on the relative level and with regard to the aspect of appearance (*snang cha*). Purity, according to Mahāyoga, is the relative truth, and even with regard to the aspect of appearance everything is taught as, and must for Rongzom be established as, pure. Thus, Rongzom's central project in *Establishing Appearances as Divine* is exactly the establishment of the present appearances as purity. Again, recall the way Mipham (see chapter 4.5) underscores the need for the valid cognition of pure seeing (*nam dag dag gzigs tshad ma*) that can establish purity with regard to appearances at the level of the relative truth.

253 See chapter 4.4 for a presentation of the two proofs.

254 "Imputed forms" (*kun brtags pa'i gzugs, parikalpitarūpa*) are set forth in the Mahāyāna abhidharma and generally described as illusory phenomena, such as appearances in a dream or reflections. They are categorized as forms that belong to the source of mental phenomena (*chos kyi skye mched pa'i gzugs, dharmāyatana*). See *Abhidharmasamuccaya*, 5a.

255 *'brel ba, pratibandha.*

256 See n. 250.

257 I have been unable to find the source of this story.

258 Thus Rongzom begins his gradual establishment of purity. Here he emphasizes the need for establishing the validity of a commonly agreed upon subject (*dharmin*), without which there would be no basis for investigation and debate.

259 It is interesting that Mipham, in his *Beacon of Certainty* (31), refutes the idea that water and pus possess the shared characteristic of fluidity. When consulting the Nyingma Khenchen Padma Sherab of Namdroling Monastery in South India regarding this issue, he reconciled the apparently contradictory accounts in the following way: Rongzom's assertion that fluidity is the common characteristic of both water and pus considers simply how water and pus both undeniably display such characteristics from the perspective of humans (and, supposedly, hungry ghosts). Mipham refutes the assertion that fluidity is the common characteristic of what the six classes of sentient beings separately perceive as pus (in the case of pretas), water (in the case of humans), amṛta (in the case of gods), etc. He argues that fluidity cannot be the common characteristic because beings in the formless realm (*gzugs med mkhams, arūpadhātu*), for instance, do not perceive any such fluidity. Thus Rongzom's example, which considers only the human perspective, is not in conflict with Mipham's position.

260 We may generally conclude that on the level of Mahāyoga anything perceived as impure is a delusion and has thus no ontological bearing. Lochen Dharma Śrī, moreover, explains that even according to the external tantras any perception of impurity or delusion pertains to the level of the false relative truth (see n. 67).

261 For a detailed discussion of the meditation on the repulsiveness (*mi sdugs pa, aśubha*) of things, see Rongzom's *Commentary to the Garland of Views as Oral Instructions* (*Collected Works of Rongzom,* vol. 1, 330).

262 According to the *Abhidharmasamuccaya,* mastered forms (*dbang 'byor ba'i gzugs, vaibutvikarūpa*) are, like imputed forms, a particular within the source of phenomena (*chos kyi skye mched kyi gzugs, dharmāyatana*). Mastered forms refer to forms attained through gaining mastery of meditation (*Abhidharmasamuccaya,* 5a). The above-mentioned "completion of the sources" (*zad par kyi skyed mched*) is such a transformed manifestation of one's form (*gzugs, rūpa*) based on having gained mastery of meditation.

263 Rongzom must prove to the opponent that there is a presence of a single commonly acknowledged subject (*dharmin*), for the entire argument will fail if a subject that is equally acknowledged by both parties in the discussion cannot be established. Such a "common subject" (*chos can thun mong ba*) is an absolute prerequisite for svātantraprayoga.

264 The Sichuan edition (1999: 566) here meaninglessly reads: *gal te de yang dag go na/*

265 Rongzom, in explaining his gradual establishment, continuously emphasizes the presence of a commonly accepted subject.

266 Wisdom (*ye shes*) refers here to the subject while the intrinsic nature (*chos nyid*) indicates the object. Mantra in the Nyingma tradition is often distinguished from Sūtra with regard to the subject's realization (see n. 98). While intrinsic nature, the object realized, is the same in both Sūtra and Mantra, the difference in view comes about through the varying degrees of subjective realization.

267 This sentence shows implicitly the relative nature of the perception of purity.

268 Rongzom explains different types of habitual tendencies: 1. *'dzin pa gnyis kyi bag chags,* 2. *dkar po las kyi bag chags,* 3. *bdag tu lta ba'i bag chags,* 4. *mngon par brjod pa'i bag chags,* and 5. *sri pa yan lag gi bag chags.* Among these five habitual tendencies (*bag chags*), Nagao lists (Nagao (1994), vol. 2, 109) *mngon par brjod pa'i bag chags* and the *srid pa yan lag gi bag chags* as occurring in the *Mahāyānasaṁgraha.* As for the former three types of habitual tendencies (*bag chags, vāsana*), it remains unclear what sources Rongzom may have relied on for his enumeration.

269 When all habitual patterns are purified there is, we might interpret, no basis for the conventions of impure and pure. As Rongzom later clarifies, wisdom (*ye shes*) transcends all extremes of existence, nonexistence, etc., and thus within the complete exhaustion of habitual patterns there is no basis for either impurity or purity.

270 Rongzom uses this term, "the pure wordly wisdom of enlightenment" (*sangs rygas pa'i dag pa 'jig rten pa'i ye shes*), frequently throughout his writings. For Mipham's account of Rongzom's controversial stand regarding the nature of wisdom (*ye shes*), see his introduction to Rongzom's *Collected Works* (*Collected Works of Rongzom,* vol. 1, 18-19).

271 Thus Rongzom concludes that as long as obscurations have not yet been purified we may establish the presence of commonly perceived subjects (*chos can mthun mong*

ba), yet once the full purification of habitual patterns has occurred the very basis for a commonly perceived subject (*dharmin*) falls away.

272 Notwithstanding his commitment to purity, Rongzom here appears to relinquish the notion of both pure and impure appearances. We might interpret his statement as implying an Atiyoga perspective where, due to the fact of primordial purity (*ka dag*), any conditioned appearance of purity as perceived on the path is still an adventitious appearance and thus not the actualization of the primordial condition (*gdod ma'i gnas lugs*).

273 Thus indicating the existence of other versions of *Establishing Appearances as Divine* (see chapter 1).

274 I am indebted to Gene Smith for much of the historical information regarding the editions of *Establishing Appearances as Divine.*

275 According to Gene Smith, Chimey Rigdzin may have incorrectly identified the Sung Thorbu (*Gsung Thor bu*) as stemming from the Palpung (Dpal spungs) prints. (Personal communication, March, 2004)

276 According to Gene Smith, there may still be other extant editions of *Establishing Appearances as Divine*, such as a one-volume manuscript recently described in the Potala catalogue containing a fourteen-folio manuscript of *Establishing Appearances as Divine* (p. 475 of the *Rnying ma'i gsung 'bum dkar chag*, Lha sa : Po ta la, 1992). (Personal communication, March, 2004)

277 According to Gene Smith, the blocks appear to have been kept at Dzogchen Monastery. There may have been prints as well at the Shechen (Zhe chen) and Gonchen (Dgon chen) Monasteries in Kham.

278 Mipham's index (*dkar chag*) is included in the *S* edition and the *C* edition of Rongzom's *Collected Works.* It is found as well in the Bhutanese edition published in 1976.

279 Whether the omissions in the *CR* are accidental or already existed in the copy that was the basis for it is hard to determine, but I am inclined to believe the first.

280 *CR* omits the double *shad* (*gnyis shad*) after all *rdzogs tshig* and lines of verse. Since it does this consistently I have not indicated this constant feature in the footnotes.